P9-DDJ-711

The

Alliluyev Memoirs

The Alliluyev Memoirs

RECOLLECTIONS OF SVETLANA STALINA'S
MATERNAL AUNT ANNA ALLILUYEVA
AND HER GRANDFATHER SERGEI ALLILUYEV

Translated and Edited by
DAVID TUTAEV

G. P. Putnam's Sons, New York

ACKNOWLEDGMENT

The last illustration in the book (of Nadezhda Stalin) is reproduced by permission of the copyright owner, Radio Times Hulton Picture Library, London.

Library of Congress Catalog
Card Number: 68-21917

PRINTED IN THE UNITED STATES OF AMERICA

Contents

Preface

THE ALLILUYEV MEMOIRS PROVIDES THE ONLY AUTHENTIC document of a family which was closely connected with Stalin throughout the two turbulent decades before the Russian Revolution, and they contain the sole human narrative of Stalin himself and his relatives ever to be published in his lifetime. These memoirs have now been supplemented by the account* given by Svetlana Alliluyeva, the daughter of Stalin and Nadezhda Alliluyeva, who figures in these memoirs.

The two memoirs, published in 1946 under their Russian titles of *A Travelled Path* by Sergei Alliluyev (Stalin's father-in-law and his daughter's grandfather) and *Reminiscences* by Anna Alliluyeva (the aunt), are here compiled into one book. This has been done both for the convenience of the non-Russian-speaking reader, and because many of the events leading up to 1907, where Sergei Alliluyev's book ends, are described and commented upon by both authors.

Not unexpectedly, the fate of these memoirs was closely linked with the tragic destiny which overwhelmed almost the entire Alliluyev family who, although they survived the Bolshevik Revolution which they had helped to bring about, were later subjected to the full rigors of Stalin's friendship. The extent of his brutality to a family which had fed and sheltered him during his days as a obscure Caucasian revolutionary and later when he stood closer to the centers of power has some-

* Svetlana Alliluyeva: *Twenty Letters to a Friend.* New York, Harper & Row, 1967.

thing of the fascination of a Russian fairly tale or, on a more elevated but equally frightening plane, some of the aspects of a Greek tragedy. Every one of the Alliluyevs who figures in these memoirs suffered from his connection with Stalin in one degree or another. Only Olga and Sergei Alliluyev, the parents, died what might be described a "natural death." Stalin's sense of filial piety, however poorly developed, drew back from inflicting on them the cruel wounds which fell on their children, their marriage partners and friends.

Sergei Alliluyev died in 1945 shortly before the publication of the first part of his memoirs in 1946 (some parts of his second volume were reproduced in the Soviet periodical press). The appearance of his book was greeted with the encomiums reserved for someone who had been close to Stalin in the early stages of his career. Similar panegyrics were heaped on Anna's memoirs, which appeared at about the same time. The two books had survived the ministrations of the official censors without whose scrutiny they would not have seen the light of day.

On the surface, at least, neither of the books had dented the carefully constructed legend, so frequently rewritten and embellished, which had grown around the dictator. The names of all "enemies of the people," persons who had figured prominently at one stage or another of his lifetime, such as Bukharin, Zinoviev, Trotsky and numerous others, had been expurgated.

Indeed Anna Alliluyeva had been assigned the expert services of an editor, Nina Bam, whose name figures on the back of the title page. This editor, if Svetlana Alliluyeva's evidence is to be taken into account,* rewrote most of these memoirs in the flat, terse style favored

* Svetlana Alliluyeva, *op. cit.*

by contemporary Soviet journalism of the day. Very little of Anna's warm, intensely human personality survived.

Nevertheless every precaution had been taken to make the memoirs acceptable, and they could have been confidently expected to sink into the effluvia of "permitted" literature, where they would rest forgotten by everyone except perhaps the specialist. Then the unexpected happened. About two years after the appearance of Anna's memoirs, a savage attack was mounted on her and her book in the official Party newspaper *Pravda,* written ostensibly by Fedoseyev but bearing all the hallmarks of Stalin's own phraseology, as his daughter now reveals.

Before we describe the storm and its attendant horrors which broke over the unfortunate Anna's head, it may be useful to consider the reasons for Stalin's ire. These lay in the recesses of his conscience and his pathological distrust of all human goodness and forgiveness.

Sixteen years had elapsed since the suicide of his second wife, Nadezhda Alliluyeva, in 1932. The rumors surrounding her death had been gossip not only in the Soviet Union but in numerous foreign publications and the press. The aging dictator who had emerged triumphantly from the Second World War, having added numerous satrapies and lands to his broad acres, could not endure even the small, expurgated voice of this middle-aged woman. Even the affection and admiration which Anna Alliluyeva showered so liberally on him were tinged with hidden barbs which struck the sensitive areas of his ego. There was no room for this Cordelia at the court of the maddened Lear, where the ghosts of the past proclaimed his own mortality, his weakness and his stultifying cruelty.

But, not surprisingly, it was not so much what Anna

Alliluyeva wrote—this will be considered in due course —but what she left out which stung him to such paroxysms of fury and revenge. The Soviet reader, long trained to read between the lines, would instantly note the omissions and draw his own conclusions.

There were also more cogent reasons for Stalin's anger. Anna Alliluyeva had not only suffered the suicide of her sister Nadezhda, but her husband Stanislav Redens, a Latvian Communist connected for many years with the Cheka (secret police), had been purged in 1938. This was known in the closed Kremlin circle to which Anna herself belonged although she refused to believe in the fact of her husband's death (she fondly imagined right up to the end of her life that Redens had been exiled to the "far north" where he had raised another family). Even Stalin's brutal assurance to Anna that her husband had been shot did not shake her own version of her husband's fate. And now here she was, this Anna Alliluyeva, who had washed, scrubbed and cooked for him in his early penniless days, breathing her noxious Christianity (repeatedly attested by her niece Svetlana), however disguised, in the pages of her memoirs.

It is small wonder therefore that Stalin, according to his daughter's testimony, exploded in the privacy of his home at Anna's all-forgiving Christianity, calling her a fool, lacking in all principles, whose goodness was worse than any evil.*

But there were more concrete reasons for his anger than we have so far been able to adduce. Anna Alliluyeva not only had the temerity to castigate Stalin (however obliquely) for his neglect of his mother, Ekaterina Djugashvili, but she also left the reader to draw his own conclusions from the fact that Stalin did not place a

* Svetlana Alliluyeva, *op. cit.*

cross over his mother's grave. A simple granite plinth with her name stands over her grave in St. David's Cemetery, and Ekaterina Djugashvili, like Anna, was a devoted Christian all her life.

Anna Alliluyeva also revealed why "the greatest military leader of all time," as Stalin was hailed, had been refused for military service during the First World War. He had suffered from an infection in his left arm which had not properly healed and he had difficulty in bending his elbow (his left arm was two or three inches shorter than the right, a fact which no official photograph ever established). Stalin explained his rejection for military service on political grounds: he was too dangerous a revolutionary to be admitted into the ranks of Tzarist recruits. This may well have been the case, although nothing would have been easier than to dispose of this inconvenient firebrand in a penal battalion, a device which Stalin himself employed in dealing with suspects and political prisoners in the last world war.

But more striking perhaps than this irksome revelation were the accounts which Anna Alliluyeva gave of Stalin's frequent arrests, banishments and escapes. Many of these were taken verbatim from Stalin's own mouth, and the observant reader is immediately struck by the relative mildness of these sentences as compared, for example, with the far more savage conditions which prevailed in his concentration camps. There were hardships and deprivations in plenty, but there was also time, it appears, for reading and writing, with fishing expeditions and hunting thrown in, all of which must also have struck the reader as something of an exercise in nostalgia.

Then there is also the fulsome letter which Stalin wrote to Anna's mother, Olga, in which he thanked her for a parcel of food and clothing which the Alliluyevs had sent him. The letter contained nothing derogatory—indeed, it showed some sensitivity on Stalin's part since he asked Anna's mother not to go to further expense on his behalf ("you need the money")—but it did show Stalin's dependence on others at this time of his life. The Alliluyevs continued to send him parcels and money, most of which they raised from their friends and sympathizers, as Anna points out. This intimate letter from Stalin was the only one to be published in his lifetime and succeeded in irritating him even further.

Despite every precaution taken by the censors, Anna Alliluyeva's memoirs are studded with examples of Stalin's ruthlessness and cunning, which the reader may find interesting to discover for himself. She makes much of his gift of mimicry, his devastating power of laughing at others, and the brief scene she describes when Stalin acted as Lenin's barber (he shaved off Lenin's beard and moustache when the latter fled disguised to Finland after the abortive Bolshevik revolt of July 1917) must have fallen within the category of "impermissible familiarity" to himself and other Soviet leaders.

But it was Anna's splendid innocence, her complete serenity and lack of fear, which infuriated him most. When she was told of Stalin's anger at her memoirs, her reaction, her niece tells us, was to laugh and to say that she would continue with the second part of her book (the present memoirs end with the Bolshevik Revolution in 1917).

Anna Alliluyeva did not succeed in writing her companion volume. In 1948 she was arrested and condemned to the barbarous sentence of ten years' solitary imprisonment and her memoirs were banned. Among others in the prison was the widow of another of Stalin's relatives, his brother-in-law Pavel's wife, Evgenia. This unfortunate widow was accused of "poisoning" her husband, who by all accounts had died of a heart attack at the height of the purges in 1938. All this is chronicled in Svetlana Alliluyeva's arresting and moving book.

By the time Anna Alliluyeva was released in 1954, both her oppressors, Stalin and Beria, were dead. She herself had spent part of her prison sentence in the prison infirmary, suffering from an incipient form of schizophrenia (with which her mother's sisters had been afflicted). Her clouded mind improved with the passage of time, and in the years before her death she became again what she had always been: a friend to all those in distress. She died in August 1964.

The circumstances of her death and her niece's moving epitaph deserve to be noted.

During Anna Alliluyeva's last illness she was taken to a country hospital reserved for the higher echelons of the Kremlin. Here she asked that the door of her sickroom be left open since she had developed a not unnatural fear of closed doors, dating from her imprisonment. Whether it was out of forgetfulness or impatience with an old woman's foibles, the door to her sickroom was locked. The following morning Anna Alliluyeva was found dead.

A more pious age will raise a cross over her remains or to her memory, but the last word must remain with her niece, who describes Anna Alliluyeva as a true daughter of Russia, a typical product of classical, Dostoyevskian Russia.

The other author, part of whose reminiscences are included in this volume, is Sergei Alliluyev, Anna's father. The reader will quickly detect a difference both of approach and style in these two memoirs. Sergei Alliluyev's writing is more direct, more affirmative, and less given to chronological meanderings than his daughter's.

Despite the easy familiarity with which he refers to his son-in-law Stalin, particularly in the use of his nick-names, he is careful to observe all the accepted rules of hagiography: Stalin's preeminence in the political tur-moil in the Caucasus is given undue weight, especially in the early days when he was barely known except to a small closed circle; his role as a strike organizer is also exaggerated. All this is to be expected, but in the fore-word to his reminiscences Sergei goes out of his way to give his "heartfelt thanks" to Stalin, who, he says, en-couraged him in his literary endeavors. He also ex-presses his thanks to a friend of even longer standing, M. I. Kalinin, who became "President" of the Soviet Union, an honorary post he held until his death. Other names which are introduced into the foreword also deserve mention; prominent among these is that of Andrei Zhdanov, who until his death in 1948 was regarded both inside and outside the Soviet Union as Stalin's putative heir. It was Zhdanov, it will be recalled, who led the "cultural" and ideological purges to cleanse Soviet liter-ature and art from "decadent Western influences."

And finally, Sergei Alliluyev quotes a brief extract from a letter sent to him by the doyen of Soviet litera-ture, Maxim Gorky (dated September 23, 1931), where Gorky expressed his interest in Alliluyev's memoirs, stating, "I strongly advise you to continue to write. . . ."

With such sponsors Sergei Alliluyev's memoirs could not help but be a success. His daughter Anna, who helped him with his memoirs, according to Svetlana Alliluyeva, is nowhere mentioned, a fortunate omission considering the subsequent fate of her memoirs.

Sergei Alliluyev was a strikingly good-looking man, a devoted father and a good husband, who despite his numerous arrests and long periods of unemployment rose by dint of skill (he was a first-class mechanic) and Party connections to minor managerial rank. In the last prerevolutionary phase just before the Bolshevik takeover, he enjoyed a modest apartment, one room of which was reserved for Lenin and later for Stalin. It was this fact, together with his marriage connection, which gave Sergei Alliluyev some measure of immunity and an honored place in Stalin's official histories, but it gave him no special standing with Stalin when he came to plead for the victims of his son-in-law's excesses, many of whom were their mutual friends and boon companions. He died at the respectable age of seventy-nine in 1945, one of the few surviving patriarchs of the revolution he had helped to bring about.

Little need be said about the Alliluyev family which will not be found in these pages. They originated from a family of serfs in central Russia, with some clerical antecedents, judging from their name (taken from "Hallelujah"). Sergei Alliluyev's grandmother was a gypsy, from which fact his granddaughter Svetlana adduces their exotic, southern cast of features, their hunger for freedom and the nomadic life.* Another grandmother was of German settler origin, whose predecessors had come to Russia in the reign of the Empress Elizabeth. But for the reader who follows these pages, the fate of three of the Alliluyev children—Pavel, the eldest; Nadezhda, who married Stalin; and Fedya, the youngest—is of greater importance since we already know what befell Anna, the fourth.

Anna's much-admired brother Pavel served with distinction in the Red Army during the civil war, fighting against the British expeditionary force in Archangel and

* Svetlana Alliluyeva, *op. cit.*

the Bashmaks in central Asia. By the end of the 1920s, he was sent to Germany in the guise of a trade delegate, although he was in fact a military adviser in the secret negotiations between pre-Hitler Germany and the Soviet Union. The presents which Pavel sent Nadezhda's and Stalin's children from Germany were cautiously described as "coming from Leningrad" in order not to upset Stalin's xenophobic sensibilities.

On his return to Moscow, Pavel, who now had the rank of a general of tank forces, found that most of his high-ranking friends had been caught up in the purges. He appealed to Stalin on their behalf, met with no response, and died from a heart attack in his office. This was in the fateful year of 1938.

The end of the youngest brother, Fedya, was even more tragic. He was undoubtedly the most gifted of the whole family (he had been recruited into the corps élite of the Marine Guards before the Revolution because of his exceptional brilliance in mathematics and chemistry). Fedya Alliluyev had been sent to be "toughened" by Stalin's close friend Kamo (Ter-Petrosyan), whose legendary exploit in robbing the Tiflis Bank of more than a quarter of a million rubles had stirred Stalin's imagination and added much-needed finances to Bolshevik revolutionary funds. A grisly charade was played out in front of Fedya Alliluyev during which a bloody body with its heart torn out was exhibited to Kamo's pupils. Fedya Alliluyev, the brilliant student, went mad at the sight of this "game." He died a prematurely old man and a partial idiot in his sixties.

Nadezhda Alliluyeva, who married Stalin in 1919 when she was a girl of seventeen, died by her own hand some thirteen years later, as we have already noted. In Anna Alliluyeva's memoirs she appears as a small child bathed and fed by her older sister, the devoted Anna, and later as an enthusiastic student of music.

With her sisters and brothers, Nadezhda ran through the whole gamut of tribulations reserved for a child of a well-tried revolutionary like her father. She too packed parcels and collected money for exiles such as Stalin. But Anna tells us little about her sister or her character, not surprisingly since Nadezhda's death and its cause in 1932 were carefully shrouded from the public. Rumors, of course, abounded even after sixteen years when these memoirs were published, taking various forms, one more lurid than the next.

The official communiqué merely stated that Nadezhda had died suddenly and prematurely. But the editor of these memoirs can recall that when he was in Moscow in 1946, one of the most persistent rumors was that Stalin himself had killed his wife in a fit of temper. Yet another version suggested that Nadezhda had drunk a cup of poisoned coffee intended for Stalin.* A more recent exposé was provided by Elizabeth Lermolo in which it was stated that Stalin and Nadezhda had quarreled over his supposed attachment to Rosa Kaganovich.† But all these rumors and reports have been finally laid to rest through the evidence of her daughter Svetlana, who has asserted that her mother killed herself on the evening of the fifteenth anniversary of the Revolution, during which Stalin behaved in a boorish and brutal manner in front of their guests.

A final irony touched Nadezhda's death. She had killed herself with a small German Walther revolver which her favorite brother Pavel had brought her from

* See Nikolaus Basseches, *Stalin,* Staples Press, London, 1952, pp. 229–230.

† Elizabeth Lermolo, *Face of a Victim,* Harper and Brothers, New York, 1955, pp. 227–229.

Germany. Her marriage, certainly in its later phases, was not a success, but then "What marriage is happy?" Madame Molotov had asked Nadezhda shortly before her death.

More significant, however, than all this minutiae of the Stalin household is Svetlana Alliluyeva's revelation that her father's character underwent a complete change following Nadezhda's death. He regarded her suicide as a deliberate stab in the back, an attempt to strike back from the grave. In that sense, Nadezhda Alliluyeva was not only her own executioner but the unwitting cause of the deaths of multitudes of persons who fell victims to this "change" in Stalin's character.

His inner feelings apart, Stalin nevertheless raised a notable memorial to his wife on the consecrated ground of the Novodevichy Cemetery, where Chekhov, Scriabin, Rimsky-Korsakov, Soloviev and Pisemsky also lie buried. Robert Payne gives this description of the monument:

"The head of the stele flowered into a portrait of Nadezhda as she had been in her youth, her hair drawn severely back, her chin resting pensively on her hand. Out of the white marble came a face and a hand, nothing more. The white stele, on one side streaked with blue veins, was a work of exquisite refinement and taste."*

Stalin, it is said, came on a number of occasions to visit his wife's grave, but whether he came out of a sense of propriety or guilt cannot be known. Forgiveness had come to him from a soul he had abused so much. Anna Alliluyeva, in some of her darkest hours when her mind was slowly recovering from madness, said that although they now blamed everything on Stalin, it was difficult

* Robert Payne, *The Rise and Fall of Stalin:* W. H. Allen, London, 1966, p. 415.

for him, too. His life had been hard and one ought never to forget what had been worthwhile.

The Alliluyev Memoirs provides few clues to what was worthwhile in a life which by all the canons of morality was little short of a charnel house, yet Stalin did show some affection for a dog (Tishka) who was his companion in his Siberian exile; he also took the young Alliluyevs for sledge rides during one of his escape periods from banishment. Such trivia will also be found in these memoirs, but they will do little to soften contemporary judgment on a man who, like Cronus, devoured not only his friends and his children, but a whole generation of men and women. The Revolution, which annihilated its own children, also destroyed the Alliluyevs, and the trains, whether they were run by Hitler, Mussolini or Stalin, never arrived on time.

The

Alliluyev Memoirs

Chapter One

Summer, 1900

THE HOUSE ON THE NARROW LITTLE STREET IN THE suburbs of Tiflis flames like a bonfire. The tongues of fire, unendurably vivid in the dark of a southern night, lick at a nearby house. People leap out in sheer terror. Grabbing anything at hand, they run down the street. A woman comes out of a white house opposite. In one arm she clasps a four-year-old girl close to her, and with her other hand she leads a small boy, not much older, who tries to keep pace with his mother.

The girl in her mother's arms, gazing in terror at the conflagration, is myself. The fire on Batum Street in the Didube quarter in the summer of 1900 remains as the first indelible impression of my childhood.

I am awakened at night by shouts and loud, unfamiliar voices. Outside the window the wind fans the yellow flames. By the light of the fire which illuminates the room, I see my mother hastily dressing my brother. She then runs up to me and quickly pulls a dress on me. Father should be here, but he has not returned from the night shift. Suddenly he turns up, says a few hasty words, and disappears. He is hurrying to the fire where his friends, the railway depot workers, have their living quarters. The town's fire brigade does not have the men and equipment to handle the fire, so it is left to the worker-volunteers to cope with it.

Father stays at the site of the fire the whole night, bringing out children or carrying out the belongings of the fire victims on his shoulders.

I always remember that black sky and the stars toward which the fire seemed to rise: I can hear dogs whining and see people's shadows leaping away from the sparks. It is terrifying! I want to cry out, but I am hustled away. My mother takes my brother Pavlusha and me to our Granny, who lived in a little house beyond the meadow on Poti Street.

. . . The first years of my life were spent in that white house on Batum Street in the Didube quarter. I was born in Tiflis in 1896. My father's friends, at his workplace and in the revolutionary underground, were our childhood friends. The participants of the revolutionary movement in the Caucasus were M. I. Kalinin, H. Franceschi, Kirillov, Chodrishvili, his wife Melanie, Vano Sturua, Georgi Rtveladze, Rodzevich, and his wife, who later became my first teacher. I remember them all.[1]

Those evenings filled with loud arguments, readings and prolonged conversations, interspersed with guitar-playing and singing, still live in my memory.

Both I and my brother Pavlusha, who was two years older, thought that the guests came expressly to entertain and play with us children.

Our favorite was Uncle Misha [M. I. Kalinin, later President of the U.S.S.R.]. He arrived before all the others and always found time to amuse us. Our walks in the Mushtaid Park with Uncle Misha were something we especially enjoyed. He would race with us in the open spaces and alleyways and would run so fast that even Pavlusha could not catch him. Then he would shake the mulberrry trees and sweet mulberries would rain down on the grass.

We did not realize at the time that Uncle Misha, our

adventurous playmate, was an experienced clandestine revolutionary and that the workers who gathered at our apartment had much to learn from this twenty-four-year-old St. Petersburgher.

Uncle Misha—Mikhail Ivanovich Kalinin—spent his years of exile in Tiflis, where he lived in the dwelling of the worker Nazarov.

He started working at the railway depot yards at the beginning of 1900. My father recalled how this young lathe-operator came to the depot, bringing with him all his revolutionary experience, persistence and drive, qualities which distinguished a member of the illegal underground.

The word *masterskii*—"works"—was one of the first I learned to pronounce. Thereafter, "works" echoed throughout the house.

"Father is at the works. Be patient, when he returns we'll all go out for a walk," Mother would say when I was barely able to totter around the room, getting ready to greet Father.

"When Father returns from the works, I'll tell him what you've been up to," she would say when Pavlusha had been naughty.

A loud factory siren would disturb the quiet of the street.

"It's time to go to the works," Father would say.

Sometimes a whole day would go by, then a night and another day, and Father would still not return. He was still there, at the works. And Mother's brother, Uncle Vanya, and Uncle Misha and our neighbors and acquaintances, they all went to the works.

They would return home with blackened faces and greasy hands.

It must be very dark and dirty there, I thought to myself, as I watched Father struggling laboriously to remove the greasy, shiny grime from his hands and face.

Mother sometimes sent Pavlusha and me to the railway depot to take Father some food. We would run up to the gates and wait patiently outside. A long stone building with large latticed windows loomed before us. It was no use trying to peer through those dirty windowpanes. Only a deafening roar of clanking and knocking came from there.

Huffing and puffing the locomotives emerge from under the arches of the rail depot. Leaning heavily against the handrails, workmen push the turntable and the locomotive revolves obediently. They would then get underneath the wheels and work lying on the ground for a long time. It must have been very warm under that puffing train!

Father rushes home during the lunch break.

"Hurry, hurry," he tells Mother, as he sits down to table.

He races through his meal, without taking off his work-shirt. Only yesterday Mother washed that shirt with so much effort, and now it is all soiled and greasy again.

"Father, when will you come to stay with us all the time?" we ask with annoying persistence. "Let's go to the Mushtaid Park. You promised . . ."

"We'll go, we'll go," Father replies.

But we have a long time to wait.

"He's gone off to the works again."

Sometimes Father would exclaim angrily: "Who do they think we are, slaves or something?"

He returns late from work, bringing some of his friends. They sit down at the table; someone opens a book and begins to read aloud. From the corner, where Pavlusha and I have been put to sleep in Mother's bed, we can hear the reader's voice clearly.

I raise my head and stare at the people seated around the table. How kind and dear they seem to me at that moment, and how much I love my father's familiar face and his pensive eyes, which always seem to be looking somewhere out into the distance.

When the book is put aside, how soothing it is to listen to the unknown words Father and his friends exchange among themselves. How good it is to fall asleep lulled by the sound of those voices. But sometimes I lie awake for a long time. I cannot get to sleep. The voices grow louder and more insistent at the table, as if they are demanding an answer from someone.

Only later, when I began to understand the meaning of those fierce and vehement speeches, did I grasp that those who gathered at our place were revolutionaries: and that Father, our whole family, were forever linked to the idea for which they fought.

I also learned from Father about the underground work at the railway depot. In those days, the young revolutionaries Stalin, Ketskhoveli and Tsulukidze, organized secret circles among Tiflis workmen. The spirit of revolt spread among them.

Father recalled the *mayevka* (the May Day demonstration) which the railwaymen celebrated together with other Tiflis workers in 1900.

Sergei Alliluyev gives this description of the mayevka *held on the outskirts of Tiflis on April 23, 1900 (O.S.). It was at this celebration that Stalin made his first public speech. Sergei Alliluyev refers to Stalin by his Georgian diminutive of 'Soso' and gives his correct surname of Djugashvili.*[2] *Anna Alliluyeva's account follows closely on that of her father. Sergei Alliluyev writes:*

Spring returns. The outskirts of the town are covered with young silky grass and the trees are in bud. Nature rejoices.

In the middle of April we, members of the underground circles, were informed that a May Day meeting would be held the following Sunday.

Preparations for this meeting were carried out with such meticulousness and secrecy that it was apparent that its organizer was an experienced, knowledgeable person. A *mayevka,* after all, was something more than a cell meeting, where no more than ten persons met at one time. For the *mayevka* a meeting of some hundreds of workmen was planned. It was a novel and incredibly complex business. But despite the fact that so many people were involved in the preparations, the works' management was completely unaware that anything was happening.

Soso Djugashvili [Stalin], who was in charge of the arrangements, chose a group of workers whom he asked to find a suitable place for the meeting. When the site was selected, he inspected it and approved the choice. He invited one of our friends, an amateur painter, to make a red banner. On this banner the portraits of Karl Marx and Friedrich Engels were depicted, together with slogans written in Russian, Georgian and Armenian.

On the eve of the *mayevka,* a Saturday, we were instructed to make our way through Nakhalovka [a working-class suburb of Tiflis], either at night or early the next morning, in groups of two or three. Our destination was the hills where the monastery of St. Anthony was situated. Here we would be met by friends who knew where the meeting would be held.

I went accompanied by two friends. As soon as we reached the hills, we met a picket-leader. He glanced at us and asked quietly: "Give the password."

We gave him the password.

The picket indicated the way up the narrow winding path into the hills. It was still dark. Here and there a few lanterns glimmered. The pickets had equipped themselves with these lanterns which were usually carried by pilgrims making their way in the early hours of the morning to the monastery. We approached the banks of Salt Lake, some eight miles out of Tiflis.

Here, at a spot removed from the road leading to the monastery, some five hundred people had gathered. As soon as the sun had risen from behind the hills dispelling the morning mist, the crowd grew animated; unconstrained, they began exchanging lively comments and arguments. I recognized many of them. Some came from the railway depot and others from Tiflis factories.

The red banner with the portraits of Marx and Engels and its stirring slogans blazed among the trees in the sun. The "Marseillaise" rang out and was echoed back in the distance from the surrounding hills.

Like birds who had fled from their narrow cages to freedom and were singing joyously, five hundred men who had escaped to the hills also burst into a loud and thunderous refrain.

Above us the red banner waved fearlessly in the breeze. This was a new and remarkably beautiful vision! The emotion was tremendous; men surreptitiously wiped away tears of triumphant joy.

One by one the speakers clambered up on the rocky platforms. These were members of the revolutionary intelligentsia, workmen from the depot and factories. I can recall the speakers. They were Soso Djugashvili, Vano Sturua, Zachar Chodrishvili, and Mikho Bochoridze. They spoke of the significance of May Day as a day of international workers' solidarity, about the difficult working conditions in their factories, their humiliation, and the ill-treatment meted out to them by their bosses.

"We must fight for our rights," the speakers proclaimed; "we must protest, organize strikes, demand better conditions."

This was the first time we had heard such courageous words expressed at a public meeting. Loud approval and cheers rose from all sides:

"Long live the First of May! Down with autocracy!"

Returning home from the *mayevka,* we felt happy, filled with determination to struggle and conquer.

The feeling of euphoria did not last long. When Stalin and his "cells" began to organize the wave of strikes which took place in May and July of 1900 in Tiflis, the majority of the Georgian Social Democratic Party ("Messame Dassy"), headed by Noah Jordania (later President of the Georgian Democratic Republic, 1917-1921), opposed these tactics.[3] *A bitter internecine quarrel developed, which Stalin neither forgave nor forgot. Sergei Alliluyev took his future son-in-law's side. He continues his narrative up to the time of his first arrest:*

July of that year [1900] was intolerably hot. The air in the workshops was stifling. Dazed men could barely walk across the shop floors, exhausted from overwork, the stench and from the heat. Everyone wanted to finish his work and escape from this hell. When the siren finally sounded its harsh clamor, workmen sighed with relief. But this was often premature. The siren had barely begun its shaking wail when the foreman would announce: "Keep the machines running. We are doing overtime!"

The siren would come to an abrupt stop, but the electric transmitters continued humming in the workshops.

Overtime was a frequent occurrence. In some workshops a number of men stood for as long as eighteen hours at the workbenches. At first the opportunity to earn extra money was welcomed. But as the overtime system spread, so pay became smaller and smaller. In the last ten years wages decreased by about forty to fifty percent. If in the nineties turners and fitters received a ruble and a half for a day's work, now they received a ruble for a full day's work, plus two to three hours' overtime.

The turners working on carriage wheels received sixty kopecks a day. To secure a minimum living wage, every workman had to put in fifty working days a month. In other words, one had to stay for a further five or six hours at overtime. Some men did not leave the workshops for weeks on end and slept beside their machines.

The plight of unskilled laborers was even worse.

By July the workers, driven by need and despair, demanded higher rates of pay and the abolition of overtime. Not everyone understood the need for this. Some were afraid that the management would stop overtime but leave their wages at the existing level. We had to explain to them that overtime led to ill health, increased the number of unemployed, and lowered the daily wage rate. Whilst this was apparent to leading workers, the older, less educated men with large families remained unconvinced. No amount of propaganda could convince them. As a result a number of fights flared up, of a totally unforeseen nature. The more militant among the younger workers beat up some of the older men.

Things then came to a head at the end of July and several mass meetings were held at night in the nearby hills. At one of the meetings attended by the lathe operators, Mikhail Kalinin appeared. The question of a strike was discussed. Kalinin talked about the difficulties this would entail, particularly for workers with large families.

"We must face facts," he said. "While we are getting ready to strike, the police are not slumbering either. They might make a few arrests to sow confusion in our ranks. Are we ready to meet this challenge?" But before he could answer his own question a dozen men replied in friendly unison: "We are ready!"

"Yes, ye are ready," Kalinin continued decisively. "Nothing can frighten us, and nothing will. We Social-Democrats know that every struggle demands sacrifices, and that our struggle is for the cause of the working classes, the producers; it is a holy struggle."

The preparations for the strike were undertaken by the revolutionary Social-Democrats in the face of the opposition of the majority of the "Messame Dassy," who tried to break the strike. Soso Djugashvili, Ivan Luzin and Mikhail Kalinin encouraged this open struggle among the workers.

The police, as Kalinin had warned, were not sleeping. On August 1, 1900, Sergei Alliluyev was arrested. He describes the scene:

I was returning home from a secret meeting. The night was very still. The heat of the day had subsided, and the air was unusually fresh. Above the town, the starlit sky looked enormous. The street was silent and deserted, but from time to time a lonely passerby hurried along. Suddenly, policemen appeared at both ends of the street, and as they surrounded me I realized that arrest was inescapable. Among them I noticed a police inspector.

"Alliluyev?" he asked, half affirmatively, and without waiting for my reply, ordered his policemen: "Seize him!"

Anna Alliluyeva takes up the narrative again at the point when she, her brother Pavlusha, her mother and Uncle Misha go to the Metekh fortress prison where Sergei Alliluyev was incarcerated:

One has to cross the whole of Tiflis from Didube to get to the Metekh fortress. Pavlusha and I ran ahead all the way and Mother and Uncle Misha could not catch up with us.

Pausing for breath, we ask: "Is it still far to go?"

The dusty, unpaved streets of the outskirts are left behind. We cross a stone carriageway and come out onto the banks of the Kura River. It is as fast and as murky as at our Didube. High up on a hill is the Metekh fortress—the Tiflis prison.

We cross the bridge and stand in front of it. I cannot keep my eyes off the barred windows.

Crowds of relatives of the imprisoned men are milling around, but it is vain hope which brought us all here to stand under these windows.

Mother spreads a napkin on the rocks and takes out a melon from her bag. Uncle Misha bought it on our way here. We sit around in a circle and Mother cuts up the melon. Uncle Misha makes signals in the air and we observe how other hands return his signs from behind the barred windows.

But you cannot recognize a face at that distance, and

we look in vain for a glimpse of Father. Will Uncle Misha be able to convey through his signs that there is a rolled-up note which we secreted in the cooked sheep's head which we delivered for Father at the prison?

A loud shout makes us jump. Two prison guards stand before us. Mother prods Uncle Misha cautiously.

"What are all these signals about?" they ask him. "Come on, let's go."

Uncle Misha feigns surprise. He was not making any signs; he was only amusing the children, making shadow animals on the rocks. But they are not prepared to listen. They take us to the police station in a carriage.

We ascend the narrow busy streets of the Maidan district. Nearby we can hear the raucous noise from the bazaar. We must cross over the street. Our carriage stops, obstructed by a bullock cart. The road is blocked, and we notice Mother and Uncle Misha exchange glances, but the guards are oblivious to anything as they are busy yelling and quarreling with the driver. Only when we reach the police station do they perceive that Uncle Misha has disappeared.

"Who was with you?" they ask Mother.

"I was alone; alone with the children," she repeats.

She does not know anyone, she did not see anyone. Some man or another came and sat down to play with the children.

"Nobody was with us," Pavlusha repeats obstinately.

"Nobody," I say, backing him up.

They release us in the evening. We make our way home. Uncle Misha remains free!

But the police are on the watch for him. A few days later Uncle Misha is taken to prison, to the same Metekh fortress.

Chapter Two

The Family Fedorenko

MY MOTHER WAS BORN IN TIFLIS, IN THE SAME DIDUBE quarter where I spent the early days of my life. My grandfathers' house was much like any other in Didube, with an open balcony around the middle floor of the house.

There was always a great deal to do. Grandmother and her eldest daughter Olga, my mother, never ceased working: they cooked, sewed and did the washing.

Grandfather was the undisputed head of the family. His wife, a quiet woman, and his children trembled before the old man. He was always inclined to be quick-tempered and stubborn, and old age did not sweeten him. But he was hard-working and tried his hand at anything. He wanted to become rich, but something always frustrated him. His profits never increased but his debts mounted. Misfortune made him even more testy and he took it out on his family.

As his eldest daughter was growing up, a friend of Grandfather's, the owner of the local sausage shop, became a frequent caller at the house. Grandfather soon observed that his guest, with whom he shared a glass or two of beer, was casting attentive glances toward his eldest daughter. The sausage-shop owner was wealthy; it did not matter that he was old and ugly and had an artificial eye.

My mother's fate had been decided. She was not yet sixteen when Grandfather promised her to the old man. However, a young fitter by the name of Sergei Alliluyev, who worked in the railway depot, was already a lodger in the house. Grandfather did not approve of the young man's attentions to his daughter Olga. What did this penniless workman want? He had not brought her up for the likes of him.

But there was nothing Grandfather could do about it. Olga was fascinated by the young fitter. Life was not easy for her in those formative years, bounded by the same street in Didube, the house ruled by Grandfather's iron fist, the unending chores and the constant gossip of the neighbors. And suddenly young Alliluyev turned up. He was not afraid of anyone. Once, when he saw the old man raise his fist at my mother, this penniless nobody who lived in the annex dared to stop him.

"I won't let you settle your differences in this way," he told the old man firmly.

Olga noticed that her father, before whom everyone trembled, retreated in front of Alliluyev.

Then there were the tales about the daily life of ordinary folk which the young lodger told Olga when they met secretly under the acacias in Granny's back yard. These stories seemed fabulous to a girl who had never been out of Tiflis.

Many years later we heard the same tales from Father. They showed us that not everything in the world was just and good.

"My father and grandfather were both serfs," Father used to tell us.

Serfs! Father's grandmother had also been a serf. She had lost all her front teeth as a young girl; the landowner had knocked them out with his snuffbox. Father's grandfather had often been flogged in the stables. He used to show his grandchildren the deep scars on his back which had not healed, even in old age.

"But you yourself were never a serf, were you, Father?" we asked impatiently.

Father had been born six years after the abolition of serfdom[4] in the village of Ramenye, in the Novohopersk district of the province of Voronezh. The peasants' lot was not greatly improved [by the abolition of serfdom]. My paternal grandfather died early from cholera, leaving five children behind. Father himself left home at the age of twelve. He had endured enough humiliation, insults and rebukes: the kind of things children never forget. Even at that age he was proud, rebellious and defiant.

From the age of sixteen he worked as a casual laborer in various factories. He began in the Borisoglebsk railway yards and then in workshops in Yelets, Kovrov, and Ufa [towns in central Russia]. He wanted to settle in Moscow or Nizhni Novgorod but could not find work. He returned to Borisoglebsk and heard from a friend about a sunny clime where working conditions were easier—so this friend alleged.

That is how Father happened to come to Tiflis. This was in 1890. He was twenty-four years old at the time. Here he worked for a couple of years in the rail depot but left because he objected to paying a fine for striking an informer.

. . . Granny told Father of the plans Grandfather Fedorenko had prepared for my mother. She complained bitterly at his cruelty and wept at her inability to help her daughter Olga.

The day for Olga's engagement with the sausage-shop owner was fixed, but the night before the celebration the bride-to-be ran away from her parents' house with the man of her choice. She tied her few possessions in a bundle and climbed out of the window. The escape had been planned with her beloved. Grandfather's room was next door. A chained watchdog, Belchik, slept downstairs and would not allow anyone to approach. Grandfather trusted this watchdog and lay peacefully in his bed. But

Belchik had long become accustomed to the young tenant's friendly attention and did not stir when he assisted Olga to scramble out of the window.

Father's young friends at the rail depot who had helped him to elope with Olga found an apartment for the young couple. Grandfather turned up at the apartment shortly afterward carrying a whip in his hand: he would teach his daughter a salutary lesson and bring her home. But when Father opened the door Grandfather soon realized he was not the master of the situation, and there was nothing left except to make peace with the young people.

From the beginning of her married life Mother was immersed in revolutionary activities. A few days after her wedding there was a loud knock at their door. The police had arrived to look for the copy machine on which Father and his friends had printed their first manifestoes. This was in 1893.

After that our apartment was often searched. Father was arrested seven times and exiled. He escaped from exile and avoided police surveillance by frequently changing his residence, moving from one town to another. Such was our wandering life until we moved to St. Petersburg.

From our earliest years we learned the dangers and deprivations which faced those who had chosen a revolutionary's path. Even before we could speak, we knew we had to be afraid of the police, and that we had to keep quiet about the things our elders said or did at home. We knew very early what dangers lay before us.

Chapter Three

Interrogation

A WAVE OF EXCITEMENT SWEPT THROUGH DIDUBE. PEOPLE gathered in back yards discussing the event of the previous night: the wealthiest house-owner in the neighborhood, a woman, had been robbed and murdered. All the grisly details were recounted because everyone knew the murderer and his victim very well, and we stood with Grandmother in the street listening to the horrible story for the umpteenth time. There was a sudden silence.

"They're bringing him," the lads shouted.

The murderer, who was escorted by two policemen, walked head-bowed but for some reason slowed down as he approached our house. Everyone heard him say aloud as he pointed at Granny: "I couldn't raise my hand against her; I couldn't kill her!"

"Poor devil," Grandmother murmured.

. . . We always took all our troubles to Granny. She would hear us out, sympathize with us, and we would dry our tears and run off with a sticky candy in our hand, our woes left behind us.

How gentle she was whenever Father was arrested and we remained alone with Mother. Granny never passed judgment on any of her children: she was proud of them. She was also on the side of every rebel in Didube. The workmen at the rail depot liked coming to Granny, whom they regarded as their friend. And if there was anything they wanted to hide, they knew they had only to ask Magdalen Yacovlievna. She never asked any questions and her house was always open to anyone persecuted by the police. Everyone in Didube knew that, including the police.

One day a young woman turned up, with tear-stained eyes, looking very disturbed. She asked for the old woman Fedorenko.

"That's me; who sent you?" asked Granny.

"I'd like to talk to your relatives, the Alliluyevs."

My mother came out to meet the unknown girl, who informed her that she had come to Tiflis to meet her fiancé Rodzevich, but people who lived in the same house as Rodzevich told her that he had been arrested the day before and had been sent away.

She had neither friends nor relatives in Tiflis, no one to turn to. Stunned by the news of the arrest, she had gone straight to the police station to find out what had happened to him.

"But what am I to do! Where am I to go?" the girl had said out loud to no one in particular.

"Try the house of the old woman Fedorenko. Her relatives the Alliluyevs will look after you," the police inspector advised, with a touch of irony; this is how the unknown girl appeared at Grandmother's house.

All kinds of people lived in the same house. They would come together in the back yard whenever one of the tenants, a drunken carpenter, started a brawl.

"Markelov is at it again," the lads would shout, raising the alarm. The carpenter either beat his wife or attacked some passerby in the street. Only Granny knew how to control this blustering bully.

She would run out into the yard and confront him, and the drunken Markelov invariably gave way. I never knew where this frail old woman could find the strength to subdue this ruffian.

The dreaded Markelov was my personal enemy. One day while we were hiding behind a fence we saw him belaboring his wife black and blue. I do not remember exactly what happened, but my young heart suddenly filled with dismay and anger and I threw a bucket of water over Markelov. Afterward I ran off and hid each time Markelov appeared in the yard. He swore he would kill me if he ever found me.

We all knew that the Black Hundreds[5] were plying Markelov with drink and pulling him into their ranks. During Tzarist celebrations, he could be heard bellowing songs in the streets of Didube as he marched with the Black Hundreds, carrying a portrait of the Tzar.

In 1905 our street was surrounded by Cossacks for some days. One of our activist friends was hiding in the house and could not get out because of the Cossack guards. Grandmother quickly made up her mind and walked out into the street.

"Don't you know the orders?" they shouted at her. "No one's allowed into the street!"

"How long are you going to hang around here?" she yelled back, unperturbed.

The Cossacks flourished their whips at her.

"We'll pull down this lair! Come on, let's search her apartment!"

Markelov suddenly appeared from nowhere.

"Don't touch this old woman. She's not hiding anyone. I'll vouch for her. . . ."

After Grandfather's death, Grandmother was forced to look after her large family. Her eldest son was sixteen, and the youngest children were about our own age, yet no one ever heard the old woman complain or ask anyone for help. But all the poor of the neighborhood turned to her for assistance and advice.

She left Didube only on one occasion. We were living in St. Petersburg at the time and had invited her to come up to get medical treatment for her eyes. But she could not endure the St. Peterburg mist. How delightful Didube seemed to her then! How dear was her own sunny, green little street where she knew everyone and where everyone greeted her.

She was accidentally run over and killed by an automobile on Veriisky Hill [in Tiflis].

Meanwhile, Sergei Alliluyev, Anna's father, languished in the Metekh prison fortress. This was his first arrest, and he left this account of his police interrogation. Its significance was not lost on the Soviet reader, who could compare the relatively mild and clumsy treatment of the Tzarist police with the conditions which prevailed in his son-in-law Stalin's time.

Six weeks went by. As usual the iron bolt of the cell door was pulled back early in the morning, and the prison orderly entered. He poured out a mug of tea, placed a hunk of bread on the table and said: 'You're going for a trip today.'

Shortly afterward the iron bolt was drawn back again.

"Get dressed," said the senior warder, standing on the threshold of the cell. "Come on; hurry."

I was taken down the narrow labyrinthine prison corridors. After descending the stairs, passing the administrative offices, I finally found myself in a large, brightly sunlit room. Captain of the Gendarmerie Lavrov sat at a baize-covered desk, busy writing something.

"Sit down," he said, without lifting his head.

I did as I was told.

Lavrov covered the paper with quick, brisk strokes, frequently crossing out what he had written. His pen scratched mercilessly. When he had finished, he lifted his dull black eyes and said, smiling faintly: "You're Alliluyev, aren't you?" He pushed a cigarette case in my direction. "Help yourself."

"I don't smoke."

"Oh, you don't?" the police captain said. "How about some tea?"

"I've just had some."

"You probably know why you were arrested. We've no wish to keep hundreds of people in prison. We'll let you out," he continued, "if . . . if you give us the names of the strike organizers. Well, what about it?"

I looked at Lavrov's thin, saturnine face and unprepossessing figure, and felt nauseated.

"I don't know anyone," I said, barely able to control myself.

"You don't know anyone? How about these?" He held out some photographs toward me.

While I studied the photos Lavrov's eyes were upon me. He watched the expression on my face closely. I returned the photos to him, saying quietly: "I don't know anyone. I never met them."

"So you never met them. Try again, you might remember them."

These were photographs of active revolutionaries—Vladimir Rodzevich, Pavel Pushkarev and Procope Japaridze. They had all been arrested and were incarcerated in the Metekh prison.

"Can you recall them now?" asked Lavrov coaxingly.

"I do not know them."

"Where did you meet them?"

"I do not know them."

"Have you known them for long?"

"I do not know them."

"Did they come frequently to the rail depot?"

"I don't know."

"How about the seminarists? Did you meet them?"

"No."

"Who do you know among the Georgians?" Lavrov fired questions at me, hoping to confuse me.

I mentioned a number of Georgian workers who I knew took no part in revolutionary activities.

"Who else do you know?"

"No one else."

"Any Georgian Seminarists?"[6]

"No."

"I'll see you rot in jail!" Lavrov shouted in a strangled voice. "I'll make you talk!"

The public prosecutor, who had entered during the interrogation and had remained silent up until now, suddenly asked: "Do you have a family?"

I told him I had a wife and three children.

The prosecutor shrugged his shoulders, appearing to be baffled. "You're an intelligent, grown-up man, yet you treat your family so brutally. It's incredible!" he exclaimed. "Your refusal to talk may have unfortunate consequences for your family. You should try to understand . . ." Lowering his voice, the prosecutor continued: "No one will know anything about it. You name the strike leaders and we'll leave you alone."

The prosecutor's words infuriated me, but I controlled myself and remained silent. The police captain thrust the indictment at me, saying through clenched teeth: "Never mind, you'll talk." Then summoning one of his policemen, he said: "Put him in solitary."

When I returned to the cell, I was in pretty bad shape and thoroughly depressed.

Bad news reached me from outside. The management at the rail depot had sacked all workers who had failed to turn up on time. The railway police authorities also issued an order stating that all persons who had been arrested for taking part in the strike had lost the right of employment on any railway establishment in the whole of Russia.

To make matters worse, a number of landlords demanded that the families of arrested men should vacate their houses and apartments. My family found themselves in that predicament.

Chapter Four

Another May Day

FATHER IS STILL IN JAIL. WE HAVE BEEN THROWN OUT OF our apartment in the white house on Batum Street. The owner does not want to have the family of a jail-bird in his house, so we move back to Granny's house beyond the open fields on Poti Street. We have to make ourselves as comfortable as we can in two small rooms which we share with Granny, her eldest son and four daughters.

Mother finds it difficult to get a job right away, but a friend comes to our rescue. She obtains work from the hospital, sewing linen. She works all day at her sewing machine. We try to keep out of her way; there is always the open field for us to play in. But we no longer look forward to the factory siren, signaling the end of the working day. We have no one to meet on the footpath which cuts across the field, but Father's friends recognize us.

"Sergei's children," we hear them say. "Fine kids. You won't have long to wait before your father returns."

Father comes home [November 1900]. The news which greets him is pretty depressing. Everyone who took part in the August strike has been sacked. Four hundred persons were arrested by the authorities in an attempt to break that strike. Many are still imprisoned and others have been banished. Father is still under police surveillance and has to take the utmost precaution to meet his friends or go to secret meetings. His friend August Burgman finds Father a job in a small engineering concern where he himself works as a foundry foreman.

The year [1901] is a memorable one for everyone connected with the revolutionary movement in Tiflis. New people bring the ferment of ideas: among these is "Soso," as Stalin was called at this time, Lado Ketshoveli and Sasha Tsulukidze. Another name is frequently mentioned in our house, that of Kurnatovsky.[7] Father speaks of him with special regard.

Victor Konstantinovich Kurnatovsky arrived in Tiflis from exile in 1901. He spent his years of exile in the Yenisey province [central Siberia], together with Lenin, Lenin's wife, Nadezhda Konstantinovna, and Krzhizhanovsky.[8]

Father often expressed his indebtedness to Kurnatovsky for introducing him to Lenin's ideas. Kurnatovsky often spoke about Lenin. He was one of those Russian intellectuals who faithfully interpreted the works of Marx to the workers.

I must have met Kurnatovsky among Father's friends. I vaguely remember a tall, gaunt man, dressed in an unbuttoned jacket, his head bent forward to the person who was talking to him since he was hard of hearing.

I remember two other persons rather better: they were Hippolite Franceschi and Vladimir Rodzevich. They both came from that illustrious company of revolutionary intellectuals, closely linked with the underground organization in Tiflis. Pavlusha and I were always delighted whenever these pleasant guests came to visit us. We always ran to meet that handsome giant of a man Rodzevich: he was surely the tallest man in the world, taller even than Father, who seemed so big compared with our tiny, thin mother.

How happy we were when Mother washed and dressed

us and took us to Klavdia Franceschi or to Kalista Rodzevich at the end of her day's work. Everything seemed so different from our little house in Didube, starting with the beautiful, wide street where the Rodzeviches lived. And the room which the Franceschis occupied, a typical, modest small room of working intellectuals, seemed to us a veritable treasure house of fine things. There was a rocking chair, and paintings on the walls, and books with marvelous illustrations in the glazed bookcase. From these books I first learned to read. Pavlusha, who was now in his ninth year, was taught by Kalista Rodzevich.

I still remember our instructors with gratitude: they always found time for their working-class friend's children, and taught Mother new ways of sewing, and even made clothes for us, and did everything to encourage Mother.

At times when we went strolling with Mother, we passed the Franceschis' house and did not drop into the Rodzeviches' sumptuous apartment near the Veriisky Bridge. We remained playing in the little park nearby. I can still see Father, seated under a shady tree, at a little table with Hippolite Franceschi, and our dear gargantuan Rodzevich, and that other man whom Father called Victor Konstantinovich [Kurnatovsky].

Later I learned that it was here on the banks of the Kura that the secret cell held its meeting, sitting under the scented acacias, drinking cheap young wine served by the kiosk keeper.

Little did those promenaders realize that these young people sitting here on the riverbank were talking against the established order which allowed these idle, overdressed, rich people to stroll at their pleasure, that they were conspiring against the bosses, the Tzar and his minions, and preparing for the bright future of the working classes.

At the beginning of spring 1901, the Tiflis police

tracked down Kurnatovsky. He was arrested with Japaridze, Franceschi, and other comrades.

But despite these arrests, barely a month later preparations went ahead for the May Day demonstration. Father, who was working at the Ruck's factory at this time, took part in this demonstration.

Sergei Alliluyev gives this first-hand description of the 1901 mayevka *in which Stalin took a prominent lead.*

Soso Djugashvili and Victor Kurnatovsky were making preparations for the May Day demonstration. However clandestine the arrangements, the police succeeded in learning about them. We were warned to take precautions: we were certain that a clash with the police was inevitable.

It was Sunday, April 22: I went out into the street in the morning. The day was warm, with a bright sun overhead. I turned into Kirochnaya Street, passed the Veriisky Bridge, and walked up the Golovinsky Boulevard. At the end of the boulevard, toward the Vera district, many people were out taking the air. Among them I recognized workers from the rail depot and Tiflis factories.

Some of the strollers appeared to be unseasonably dressed, in heavy overcoats and Caucasian sheepskin caps. Among them, dressed in similar fashion, was Vano Sturua.

"What's the matter? Are you sick?" I asked, in astonishment.

Vano lifted his cap and smiled.

"No, I'm fine."

"Then what's the meaning of this getup?"

"Soso's orders."

"Whatever for?"

Vano came up and whispered in my ear.

"You see, I'm supposed to head the demonstration, with others. . . . Get it? We'll be the first to receive the blows from the Cossacks' whips. The coat and cap should soften the blow. You follow?"

"Yes, I follow."

"Smart, isn't it?"

It was a sensible plan, since police reinforcements had gathered in every back yard from Golovinsky Prospect to Palace Street.

It was almost noon. The time gun at the arsenal boomed out, announcing midday. Vano Sturua rushed to the head of the demonstration which was moving down the center of the street.

"Long live the First of May!" the crowd roared in unison. "Down with autocracy!" "Long live Freedom!" We marched to the center of the city, singing the "Varshovyanka" [the Polish liberation anthem]. Cossacks suddenly galloped up and the fight began. Our group was dispersed at one point, but managed by mixing with the crowd to reappear at another. All this occupied a few minutes.

The boulevard was thronged with police, Cossacks and auxiliaries. They began shoving, pushing and beating up the demonstrators and onlookers. We broke into smaller groups and made our way to the Soldiers' Bazaar, where we had arranged to meet after the demonstration.

As usual on Sunday, the bazaar was crowded, but we were an odd assortment of customers on this occasion. We approached the stalls, bargained, but went away empty-handed. By noon the stall holders knew what was up. As the time gun boomed out, the crowd began to roar out its slogans.

The police hurled themselves, with drawn sabers, on the man holding the banner. But the banner was passed from hand to hand. Whenever the police charged, the banner reappeared in a different part of the crowd. A bloody riot ensued. Cossack whips whistled through the air, sabers flashed; the workers replied with sticks and stones. It was a desperate encounter. Many workmen were wounded; the police also suffered casualties. The banner was taken off its pole and carried off by women. It is now preserved in a museum.

I was dismissed from my employment.

"You're sacked," I was told at the Ruck's factory. I had expected as much. . . .

Beria wrote that "on the eve of March 22, 1901, Victor Kurnatovsky was arrested. That very night a search was made in the Physics Observatory where Comrade Stalin was working. The search took place in the absence of Comrade Stalin. The day after the search the gendarmerie adopted a decision to:

" '. . . prosecute the said Joseph Djugashvili [*Stalin*] *and examine the accused persons on the evidence of my investigation of the degree of political unreliability of the members of the Social-Democratic circle of intellectuals in the city of Tiflis, pursuant to the State Security Act.' "*

After the search Comrade Stalin went underground.

Concerning this demonstration Lenin's Iskra *wrote in 1901* [*No. 6, July 1901*]*:*

"The event that took place on Sunday, April 22, in Tiflis is of historic import for the entire Caucasus: this day marks the beginning of an open revolutionary movement in the Caucasus."

Some time after the demonstration, Sergei Alliluyev found work at an electrical power station in Baku, through the recommendation of Leonid Krassin, a qualified engineer and an active supporter of his faction.[9]

Chapter Five

Baku 1902

THE BAILOV PENINSULA STRETCHES FAR OUT TO SEA. A hilly street runs through the promontory, joining it to the seashore at Baku. At its tip are the oil refineries of the Bibi-Eybat combine.

From the windows of our house at the electric power station we can see regular lines of oil derricks. The sea foams below the yard; on its surface thin ribbons of oil reflect all the colors of the rainbow.

Baku has been called by its Azerbaydzhan inhabitants "the city of winds" [Bakue]. Early in spring and autumn the north wind shakes the walls of the house, and sand seeps through the crannies of the closed windows, covering the sills and floors with thick layers of dust.

When the oil flamed at the borings, a black cloud obscured the sky, and thick patches of oily soot fell on the town. Trees could not grow in this poisonous atmosphere; as a result Baku lacked all greenery. This was something of a surprise for those of us who had been brought up in lush Didube.

We arrived in Baku in summer; later that autumn Nadya [Stalin's second wife] was born. Mother returned from the natal clinic and we watched, fascinated, as she swaddled the baby. Then Nadya would be given a bath and it was great fun to see her splashing about, all pink and smiling.

Father worked as a senior stoker at the power station. We saw him go off in the evening for the night shift, and we remained alone with Mother. We did not feel like going to sleep. It was hard to get used to the howling wind and the fiery glow from the oil borings. To calm our fears we asked Mother to read to us.

I remember one such occasion when the reflection from the fires illuminated the windows and a storm raged out at sea, and we all sat around the table listening to "The Caucasian Prisoner" [celebrated poem by Lermontov]. Everything felt so eerie and the poem was so sad.

Finally Mother closed the book: it was time to go to bed.

"Don't turn out the lights," Pavlusha begged.

"You should be asleep," Mother said, switching off the light.

But I could not sleep. Shadows moved in the corner of the room and the wind cried with a human voice. Pavlusha tossed beside me. I knew he was also frightened. Suddenly he let out a scream, and there was nothing we could do to quieten him.

"I'm frightened! Frightened!" he kept saying.

"Run out and fetch Father," Mother told me.

I rushed out into the street, forgetting all about the storm and the fires. The lights at the power station blinded me.

"Who are you looking for, young lady?" they asked me as the workmen began calling for Father loudly.

Pavlusha, the doctors diagnosed, was suffering from a nervous disorder. It was advisable to take him to healthier surroundings, away from the grimy, oil-laden air of Baku. Father remembered his friends the Rodzeviches, who were living at Kutais. He wrote to them and Pavlusha went to Kutais, where he soon recovered.

Only recently I revisited Baku. It is now an attractive,

well-laid-out modern city, with fine promenades, filled with flowers and tropical plants; the clean, asphalted streets run in neat, parallel lines from the center of the industrial suburbs. I did not recognize the city of my childhood. Today you are hardly aware that you are standing on rich oil-bearing soil, but in those days the oil seeped out everywhere. You had only to leave the main street and approach the industrial suburbs before you were jumping over oily puddles.

Father left the power station after a quarrel with the management at the end of 1901 and found work at the Rothschild refineries in the Black City. Today, no trace remains of this district, but in those days the Black City district was really black since it was totally enveloped in smog.

Oil pipes ran along the streets and alleyways of the Black City. You had to clamber over the pipes to cross the street and make your way gingerly along the narrow wooden duckboards which served as pavements.

Sergei Alliluyev, who was now working in the Rothschilds' oil refinery, gives this account of working and living conditions in Baku.

The workers lived in barracks, sleeping on dirty plank-beds, without taking off their working clothes. But in the barracks where the Persian workmen lived there were not even planks, and people slept on the earthen floor, on cane mats.

Medical services were badly organized. Hospital beds were few, and medicines were in short supply. There were no canteens and one had to eat in crowded Persian inns and teahouses.

Baku also had hardly any tolerable form of transport. In that large, sprawling city there was only one horse tramline. Tired, aged nags dragged the ancient open carriages at the speed of tortoises, often dropping dead from sunstroke or sheer exhaustion. Sometimes they would stop in their tracks and no amount of whipping or whistling would budge them. Passengers would jump out and push the carriages with loud cries; the horses would start to move until they came to the next incline.

The Electrosila Company, at the suggestion of R. E. Klasson (its director), suggested to the town council that an electrified tramline should be constructed, linking all the industrial quarters with the city. But the town fathers rejected the idea on the grounds that such a tramline would "cause accidents" in the narrow streets of the city. The real reason for their refusal was that a majority of town councilors held shares in the horse tramway, which was a profitable business.

In February 1902 Sergei Alliluyev was arrested for the second time and charged with being associated with a subversive organization. Apart from his left-wing friends such as Victor Kurnatovsky and Hippolite Franceschi who had been arrested earlier, the police also seized Noah Jordania and a group of his "right wing" supporters. In March, while Sergei Alliluyev stood at the window of his solitary cell, he heard a disturbance.

Suddenly there was a sound of knocking from the cell above. I opened the door of the stove. Hippolite Franceschi was calling me. I could communicate with him through the stovepipe. He said that the political prisoners who had spent a year in solitary confinement had now been moved into a communal cell. They had been starved of company and were now reveling in conversation, jumping for joy, laughing and chatting.

It is quite true that for the first few days the communal cell was alive with excitement, but this euphoria began to wear off as the impact of meeting people faded, and arguments rang out with renewed force. Among the persons arrested there were people of different political outlooks. These differences had abated at the first contact in the communal cell, but such friendship could be but short-lived.

The supporters of the majority faction of the "Messame Dassy" grouped themselves around Noah Jordania, and the minority wing sided with Victor Kurnatovsky. Basic political issues were debated. These became so heated that they finally quarreled among themselves. Silence reigned in the communal cell. No one answered my calls. For some reason, I assumed that they had all been punished and taken to detention cells. I slept badly that night.

Early next morning I again heard the familiar knocks.

"Why haven't you answered my calls?"

"We've been squabbling like mad dogs, barking and biting each other. Now we're sitting in opposite corners like screech owls in a forest, puffing and hissing at each other." The brief honeymoon was over.

One evening the knocks from above became urgent and alarmed.

"Is that you, Hippolite?"

"No, it's Luzin [Ivan Luzin: one of the arrested left-wingers]. There's bad news. . . . There's been great trouble in Batum. Arrests and shootings. Soso is among the arrested."

On March 9, 1902, Stalin had organized a mass demonstration of some 6,000 workers from the Batum factories belonging to Rothschild and Mantashev. They had met to protest against the arrest of some 32 strikers the previous evening. The police opened fire and some fifteen of the workmen had been killed. On April 5 [April 18] Stalin was arrested, together with other strike leaders. A year later, in November 1903, he was removed from the Batum jail and exiled to the Irkutsk province in Siberia. Lado Ketskhoveli took over the leadership of the left-wing Social Democrats and its illegal publication Brdzola [*The Struggle*]. *In May 1902 Sergei Alliluyev was released for lack of evidence and began working as a mechanic for various illegal publications.*

As soon as I left prison, comrades from the workshop arranged for me to meet Mikho Bochoridze. Mikho was pleased to see me.

"I need your help," he said affably. "There's a job to be done."

He passed on the instructions of the Tiflis committee of the Social-Democratic Party, telling me to take on the job of a repair mechanic at the Georgian "Friendship" printing works.

"Get to know the workers well," said Bochoridze, "and make arrangements to supply our printing works with equipment."

The Tiflis committee had, at this time, a small printing works, created by Soso Djugashvili before he left for Batum. At first the press operated in one of the Tiflis working-class quarters of Nakhalovka; then it was taken to a place not far from the funicular railway, and finally returned to Nakhalovka in Lotkinsky Street. But it was difficult to obtain the right equipment, and this was the job the committeee had entrusted to me.

Sergei Alliluyev, an expert locksmith and mechanic, did his allotted job very well. But the directing mind behind the illegal printing operations was not Stalin, but his close friend Lado Ketskhoveli, a priest's son who, like Stalin, attended the Theological Seminary of Tiflis. In 1900 Lado was sent by the Social Democratic organization to Baku.

Lado not only built up the revolutionary workers' organization but led the party in Baku; he also carried out the complex and extremely responsible task of creating an illegal printing works. At first he was supplied with a small, hand-operated press made in Tiflis, with type face, paper and printing ink for printing leaflets. But soon the

Party required a larger printing press, capable of producing an enormous output of illegal literature, and he rose to this challenge.

But in order to buy a printing press and get regular supplies of paper and ink one required a license signed by the governor. Where was one to get such a license? Lado obtained a blank license form with the official stamp of the "Yelisavetpol governor", filled it in, and signed it on behalf of the governor. The copy of the license was countersigned by a Baku notary, and thus Lado was able to obtain the necessary equipment at any time.

When all the equipment had been bought, he began looking around for the right people to run the printing works.

Finally, everything was ready. Thus the first issue of *Brdzola* [*The Struggle*] appeared. I remember how Lado ran to Krassin, beaming with joy. He took the newspaper out of his pocket, unfolded it— and said loudly:

"Look at it—this is *Brdzola*."

But the work of producing the illegal newspaper and leaflets was not without its dangers. Two "comrades" who has been deputed to carry the American type faces for the Baku press suddenly panicked when they thought they were under police observation. They abandoned at a railway station two woollen saddle bags in which the type was carried, together with plates of the portraits of Marx and Engels. Fortunately the station guard took the bags to the luggage depository, from which they were recovered by a friendly inspector at the locomotive depot. In the summer of 1903 it was decided to expand the Tiflis printing works.

Mikho Bochoridze chose the site of the [new] illegal printing works; it was a vacant plot of land in Avlabar, on the outskirts of the city. He obtained permission from the town authorities in Tiflis to build a house. To begin with, the entire plot was surrounded by a high fence, and then deep foundations were dug by stonemasons employed for this purpose. When the lower part of the foundations and the walls had been completed, the workmen were told that the owner of the house had gone bankrupt so all work would cease, and only a few trusted workmen were left on the site.

A stone arch was built over the walls which had already been erected. Thus a large cellar was created in which the printing press was installed. A small opening was left in the arch and the entire ceiling covered with a thick layer of earth. Over this crypt they built a two-story house, and when this was completed, a well was sunk, connecting it with the cellar. Two wooden ladders were lowered into the well, covered with heavy beams, which were also covered with earth. Another well was sunk close by, linked to the first well by a tunnel. The entrance to the printing press was through this second well, which was circled by a wall and had an awning, giving the appearance of a kind of shed.

The Tiflis organization entrusted me and Lelashvili [Gigo Lelashvili, Alliluyev's assistant] to equip this press, and it was for this purpose that I was employed at the Georgian "Friendship" printing works.

The Avlabar press survived until April 1906. In April the police, together with secret agents, paid a surprise visit to the works. They searched the yard and all the rooms in the house but found nothing. Just when they were about to leave, one of the agents noticed some waste paper among the weeds. He set one of these pieces alight and threw it down the well. The paper fluttered for a short distance, but was then drawn to the side by the draft from the cellar. The agent then lowered a fireman on a rope into the well and he found the secret entrance to the cellar, which is how the Avlabar printing works came to be discovered.[10]

Chapter Six

Lado

In the spring of 1903 Sergei Alliluyev was warned that he was under police surveillance. He immediately left his employ with the "Friendship" printing works and found work as an assistant foreman on the construction of the Baku-Batum pipeline. A general strike was brewing in the Transcaucasus, but Alliluyev made preparations to enter a hospital for the removal of a tumor on his right breast. He was arrested again in July.

FOR THE THIRD TIME I FOUND MYSELF IN THE METEKH prison. Here I discovered Lado Ketskhoveli, who had been arrested in Baku in September 1902. With him in prison were Victor Kurnatovsky, Hippolite Franceschi, Sylvester Jibladze and others, who were waiting transportation to Siberia.

I was given a cell overlooking the exercise yard.

One day toward the end of July, during the morning exercise, I saw a group of convicted criminals attack and wound Demidov, another prisoner. Demidov, who had once been a high-ranking civil servant but had been sentenced for bribe-taking and forgery, now worked as a clerk in the prison office. He was often asked by the criminal prisoners to write official letters, appeals and letters on other juridical matters. Someone discovered that Demidov betrayed the secrets entrusted to him to the investigating authorities, which was the reason behind the attack.

After a short while I was moved into another cell on the third floor, with a view of the River Kura. Immediately below me was Lado Ketskhoveli's cell, and next to me was the "solitary" in which Vano Sturua had been incarcerated.

Since we were in such close proximity, we began to communicate with one another. I informed my comrades about the Demidov business, but Lado already knew all about it.

Lado had managed to establish contact with illegal organizations through the help of one young criminal who had been sentenced to hard labor and exile. This young fellow worked in the prison printing shop and from time to time he passed clandestine literature to Lado, who, in turn, handed him letters to be sent outside. The typesetting works were on the first floor of the political section of the prison, but the printing works were located right under Ketskhoveli's cell.

At night, when the young convict was left alone in the typesetting works, he gave Lado a prearranged signal. Lado would then lower to the first floor a thin rope to which the man attached newspapers or letters addressed to Ketskhoveli. Lado "mailed" his letters in similar fashion.

On the eve of the attack on Demidov, Lado gave him a letter for one of his trusted friends. This letter was written in Georgian and in it Lado made inquiries about the progress of illegal organizations in Baku. But the young convict was unable to pass this letter to his outside contact and took it with him into his cell. After the attack on Demidov the next morning, the prison warders searched the cells for weapons and discovered Lado's letter.

That morning Lado did not reply to our signals. Nor did he answer the signals on the following day. We grew alarmed. Only later did we find out that Lado had been sentenced to seven days in a dark solitary cell for spitting in the prison governor Milov's face and for pushing him out of his cell.

On his return from solitary, Lado told us: "Milov came to see me and I asked him to return my letter. How stupid of me! And what was Milov's reaction? He merely grinned. . . ." Lado said nothing about the fact that he had pushed Milov out of his cell.

His spell in solitary did not break his indomitable will. He continued his fight against prison regime, fomenting strikes and riots. The prison threatened to burst its seams and discipline dropped. Seeing that Lado was behind all this unrest, the prison authorities demanded that he should be transferred to a military prison, and meanwhile they deprived him of exercise and took away his books and his bed.

One morning Lado started to sing the "Marseillaise." He sang loudly, forcefully, until all the prisoners followed suit one by one. The prison administration panicked. Warders rushed from cell to cell, yelling: "Be quiet! Be quiet this instant!"

But the song grew in fervor, and when it finally ended a fierce shout came from Lado's cell: "Long Live Socialism!"

The prison administration decided to settle with this insubordinate revolutionary. On August 17, Lado as usual began calling to the other prisoners. He stood on the windowsill, holding tightly to the thick iron bars and began exchanging loud comments with his friends. At that moment a group of Armenian shepherds appeared on the opposite bank of the Kura. They had come to look for relatives and fellow villagers in the prison. Lado, who knew Armenian perfectly, began calling to them.

As I happened to be sitting on the windowsill in my cell, I saw everything which followed.

An armed prison guard who saw Lado at his window blew his whistle. The officer of the guard hurried up to him and, pointing at his rifle, said something. The guard took aim.

We all began shouting to Lado to get down from the window. A shot was heard, followed by silence; the silence may have lasted for some minutes, but perhaps it was only seconds. Nothing further was heard from Lado.

"Lado! Lado!" Voices were heard on all sides.

But there was no answer. Shouts and yells could be heard from the prison cells; the entire place was in an uproar.

"Lado has been killed!" I heard people exclaim. I paced up and down my cell completely lost and bewildered, refusing to believe that Lado was no longer among the living.

Police Inspector Kovalev appeared in the prison some time afterward. He went around the cells assuring everyone that Ketskhoveli had only been wounded and would survive. But on the following day the terrible news passed from one cell to the next: Lado was dead. A bullet had pierced his heart, and he had been killed instantly.

Thus perished one of our best revolutionary comrades, a glorious son of the Georgian people, one of the closest friends and companions in arms of Soso. Eternal memory be his!

In September 1903 Sergei Alliluyev was again released from prison and found work in the oil refineries of Baku. In August of the same year the Second Congress of the Russian Social Democratic Party was held in London at which Lenin and his "majority" (Bolsheviks) split with Martov's "minority" (Mensheviks). Reconciled in 1905, they finally split at another London Conference in 1907, which Stalin attended.[11]

In December 1903 Sergei Alliluyev and another fellow conspirator were ordered to Tiflis to bring back a hand printing machine to Baku. He came to collect a part of this machine which had been hidden in the apartment of Mikho Bochoridze.

Mikho was not at home. I was greeted by his aunt Babe Bochoridze.

"Mikho has gone out," she said. "I don't know when he'll return. He didn't say anything."

"Mikho will soon be back," I suddenly heard a masculine voice exclaim.

I looked around. A young man of about twenty-three or twenty-four entered from an adjoining room.

"He's one of us," said Babe, pointing to me.

"One of us?" the young man repeated, inviting me with a gesture into the other room.

Having seated me at a table, the young man—Soso Djugashvili—asked: "Well, what good news have you to tell me?"

Soso Djugashvili had only recently escaped from Novoya Uda in Eastern Siberia, where he had been exiled for three years. He had tried to escape in the first few days of exile, but had to give up the attempt because he lacked any warm clothes. His face and ears had become frostbitten and he was forced to return. On January 5 [1904] he made his successful getaway.

Mikho returned soon and we began to talk together. Koba[12]—as Joseph (Soso) Djugashvili was now called—took an eager part in this conversation. He asked me what kind of printing machine we had obtained and how it had been packed. I told him that we had packed the printing cylinder [drum] in a soft wicker basket and covered it with provisions.

"A splendid idea," Koba confirmed. "But how are you going to take it?"

I told him that I and Shelgunov [a friend] were going to sit in the same railway carriage.

"That won't do. One of you should take the drum, and

the other the remaining parts. Sit in separate carriages and don't contact each other."

"As for the type face," he said after a brief pause, "we'll send that along by another comrade a short while afterward."

This is Sergei Alliluyev's account of his first meeting with his future son-in-law Stalin.[13] *Shortly afterward he left Baku in search of work in central Russia. In October 1904 he brought his family from the Caucasus to Moscow. Anna Alliluyeva describes the events there.*

Chapter Seven

Moscow 1904

Moscow welcomed us coldly. In November frosts appeared, to which we were unaccustomed.

. . . We shiver in our light Tiflis overcoats. When snow covers the streets we cannot summon up courage to go out in our galoshes. We have neither furs nor "valenkis" [felt boots]. The family is poverty-stricken. Father is out of work. Casual labor brings in a small income on which we barely survive. And the police continue to follow Father, who cannot get permanent employment.

It is impossible to keep warm in our unheated room in Volkovo Lane in the Presna district. Father lies ill in bed, from an attack of rheumatism. I sit beside him, glancing sideways at Mother. She is at the table, feeding Nadya with a spoon. I should like to say something which lifts the hopeless crestfallen expression on her face, something to make Father stir as he lies there silent with his face turned to the wall. But what can one say? The police continue to watch him and he cannot find work. How cold it is in Moscow! Why were we forced to come so far? I remember sunny Didube and the warm seashore at Baku. It is bitterly cold in the room.

"Remember the sea?" I whisper to Pavlusha.

What else is there to talk about? How can one break

the silence? Suddenly there is a ring at the door. Who could that be?

"Sonya has come!" the boys shout. Sonya Lepinskaya is one of the new friends we found in Moscow.

There were others, such as the family Nikiforov, the Hrenkov girls, the journalist and Bolshevik Vassily Panov—these were Russian revolutionaries with whom Father made friends in Moscow. All of them suffered a tragic fate.

Our new friends the twelve-year-old Valya and ten-year-old Sonya Hrenkov played with us in the house of the Nikiforovs.

"Their mother's in prison. . . . She's a revolutionary. . . ." Pavlusha told me.

Valya and Sonya's mother committed suicide in prison. Her friend, another woman prisoner, had been birched by the warders. In protest against this insult, she poured paraffin on her dress and set fire to herself. Her death was reported in underground booklets.[14] One of these fell by accident into the hands of her daughters, who had not been told of their mother's death. The shock was so overwhelming that Sonya, the youngest, fell ill with meningitis and for a long time lost her sight and hearing.

It was always noisy and gay at the Nikiforovs. They were fond of children and knew how to entertain them. We cannot wait for Mother to take us to their place. Their youngest son Sergei is the same age as ourselves, but the elder, the twenty-year-old Sasha, not only invents new games for us but takes a leading part in them.

Poor Sasha! He was not fated to live long, yet he was full of the joy of life. The older Nikiforov brothers were constantly in and out of prison even at that time. Sasha was arrested in January 1905, after the event on the Winter Palace Square in Petersburg.[15] On the day following the demonstration he was banished to Nizhni Novgorod [now Gorky], where he was hanged for shooting at a secret police officer who had insulted the prisoners. I remember Sasha on the last evening before his arrest. He came to see us and we greeted him jubilantly as usual.

"Let's play a game, Sasha! What shall we play?" we said, tugging at him.

Sasha's mind seemed to wander and he appeared sunk in gloom.

"Sasha, what's the matter?"

"Well, it's just that . . ." he said, looking affectionately at us, "I dropped in for a moment. I must go away. It's sad to say goodbye."

We did our best to console him.

"Yes, of course, but you'll come back soon, Sasha. Don't stay away too long."

"Yes, yes, I shall be back," said Sasha staring at us. "I'll be back. Wait for me. . . ."

But he never returned. A few months later his executioners in Nizhni erected a scaffold for Sasha. His two elder brothers also perished in prison.

. . . But in the room in the Presna district it is as cold as ever. Life goes on as usual. Father still goes out looking for work, but by the end of December 1904 he is still unemployed. But why does he come home so late? He spends a long time talking to Mother.

"The movement is growing. Our strength increases. A storm is brewing. We won't have long to wait, Olga."

We had grown accustomed to guessing the meaning behind those words. It was good to hear them!

. . . But there is an air of gloom in the room in the Presna district. Mother falls ill. Sonya Lepinskaya comes to help out. One day she turns up looking very cheerful.

"Olga Eugenievna, I want to make a suggestion. Things are very hard for you while Sergei is out of work. How would you like to come as housekeeper in a students' communal apartment? You could all live there. . . ."

So in the new year of 1905 we moved to the apartment

on the fifth floor in Vladimir-Dolgoruky Street. Beds were placed for us in a tiny room at the end of the corridor.

On January 5 we first went to sleep in our new place. Here it was warm, not as at Presna. Pavlusha was already whispering to me: "These students don't seem a bad lot. They're real revolutionaries," he added, authoritatively.

One could hardly forget what happened on that bitter, confused evening of January 9. On that day the workers in Moscow learned of the blood which had been spilt on the Winter Palace Square. Mother put us to bed earlier than usual, but we did not complain. We sense the highly charged atmosphere of the grown-ups and try not to irritate Mother. We know that the Tzar shot at people who had come to him. Rifles and gunfire slaughtered workers, children . . .

. . . We are already tucked up in bed. Nadya and Fedya are asleep, and Pavlusha and I lie with our eyes open, without speaking. I keep imagining the blood.

"The whole square was covered in blood," our elders are saying. We can hear their muffled voices from the room next to us. I know that they are talking about the events in Petersburg. Pavlusha draws nearer to me.

"The meeting has begun already."

We strain to hear what is being said. Pavlusha gets up and tries to peer through the high window which opens on to the larger room next door. They are sitting around a table, bent over some sheets of paper. Father is writing something down. He lifts his head and we immediately dive under the bedclothes.

"They are writing manifestos," says Pavlusha. "Tomorrow they will be scattered in the streets."

On January 10, a meeting was held in our apartment of the leading members of the Bolshevik regional organization. They were getting ready to distribute leaflets calling for a strike of Moscow workers. Father was put in charge of the distribution of the leaflets, which were to be brought to him by the worker Sergei Chukayev. It was also decided at this meeting that Father should go to Tula to fetch cartridges. But since Father was under police surveillance and it would be difficult to explain his absence, Mother volunteered to go in his place.

. . . I follow Mother's brief preparations for her journey and my heart sinks.

"You'll be back soon?" I ask, unable to hold myself back.

"Yes, soon," Mother says, turning away.

She kisses Nadya and puts her to bed. Then she embraces me.

"Look after the little ones," she whispers. Her voice breaks. "You're a big girl now. Behave yourselves and don't run about the streets."

The door slams behind Mother. No one sees her off. Pavlusha and I go to our cubbyhole of a room.

"Mother has taken the manifestos with her," he says. "They will read them in Tula."

"Go to sleep. It's already getting late," I reply. Mother would have used the same words. . . .

Finally everyone goes to sleep. Time passes. . . . But what's this? I wake up.

Is it morning? I can see lights in the high window of the next door room. I hear harsh shouts, voices.

"Niura, are you asleep? What's happening?" Pavlusha nudges me.

He throws off the bedclothes. We again climb up to the fanlight. The room next door is filled with strange people. . . .

"Police! It's a search! Look! Look!"

Pavlusha edges closer to me. I follow his downward glance. There is a man on the threshold aiming a revolver. Two other men have seized Father. He is undressed. A policeman is rummaging in an open suitcase which lies on the floor. Alarm for Father and hatred for these people grips me. I fall on the bed. Pavlusha turns round, his face white as a sheet.

"What are they doing to Father? Niura, I'll go to him."

Pavlusha lowers himself back to bed.

"Stay where you are!"

What would Mother have done? I ask myself. I bend over the smaller children. Nadya and Fedya are softly and peacefully snoring in their sleep.

"Quiet, quiet, the children are asleep," I say twice over.

The voices in the room next door grow louder. I can hear Father. Pavlusha again stands frozen at the window.

"They've found something," he says, suddenly. "Niura —" he jumps down beside me. "They've found some manifestos in Mother's jacket."

"They've found them?"

I should like to climb up onto the table again to look through the window, but I can hear Father's voice at the door. I pull up the bedclothes and lie quite, quite still. Pavlusha is also motionless.

"You can't force me to leave the children unattended," Father says. "Someone has to look after them."

"Go on, take him away!" The words fall like a stone on us.

"Will they really take him away?"

Pavlusha and I take each other by the hand. The voices behind the door grow louder.

"I refuse to go!" (Could this really be Father's voice?) "I won't leave the children on their own!"

"Release him."

The door to our room is flung open. Father enters, with men standing behind him. The room is too small for them to approach any nearer.

"Papa!" Nadya cries out.

The noise has wakened the smaller children. Fedya also scrambles out of bed.

"Papa!" Nadya will burst into tears in a moment, but Father takes her in his arms, bends down to me, and whispers: "Tell Sonya to send Mother a telegram immediately. Immediately, you understand."

"Come on, get going!" they shout to him from the corridor, and Father raises his voice, saying: "Get dressed, Niura, and run for Auntie Sonya. She'll take you to her place. I must go."

I dress hurriedly, run out of the door, and dash headlong down the stairs. Sonya Lepinskaya lives in the same house, but the entrance to her apartment is around the corner. I'm sure someone's after me and that I shall be grabbed at any moment! Will I ever get there? Ah, here's the entrance. I ring the doorbell and fall straight into her arms. I don't have to say very much. Sonya seems to know everything.

"So the manifestos were found only in your mother's jacket? How many?"

"Two," I reply. "She hid all the rest in the larder on the landing."

"Good," says Sonya. "We must go back to your apartment immediately; I'll accompany you to the door."

"What about the telegram? Father said it was urgent."

"It'll all be taken care of. But not a word, you understand?"

Of course, I understand. What does Sonya take me for? I beg her to hurry: they could have taken Father away by now.

I go up the stairs alone and ring the bell. The man with the revolver opens the door and stares suspiciously at me. I run past him and go to Father. Nadya is still in his arms. Pavlusha holds Fedya.

"Sonya will come to fetch us," I say. "I told her."

I told her everything, and about the telegram, I say to myself mentally. I am sure Father can read my thoughts. I stare so hard at him. Of course he understands what I am trying to tell him. He hands Nadya over to me and says to the men: "Let's go."

They do not all leave with Father. Three secret policemen remain in the apartment. This is a trap.

Pavlusha goes to fetch some bread and milk from the

kitchen in the morning. I listen unobserved to what is being said to him.

"Your father must have hidden his books and leaflets somewhere. Show us the place."

"We've no other books except these," Pavlusha replies. He is probably indicating the table on which they heaped the books they had pulled out of the cupboard during the search of the previous evening.

"You ask your sister; she probably knows."

Pavlusha enters the room, followed by one of the guards. My brother looks at me and says: "You'll see, she will say the same thing as I did."

"Where did your father hide his books and papers? If you tell us, we'll take you to your mother."

"We haven't any books other than those in the cupboard. Father never hid anything."

That night when we were getting ready to go to sleep, Pavlusha says to me: "You know they asked me about the machine which printed the manifestos. They think it's here."

"And what did you say?"

Pavlusha shakes his fist at the door.

Next morning there is a ring at the door of the apartment.

"Who can that be? Anyone who comes here will be seized immediately," Pavlusha says.

Sergei Chukayev is at the door. He has brought some manifestos with him.

"I mistook the landing," he tells the police. "Let me go."

But they force him to undress. He had padded himself out with leaflets under his jacket. The policemen beat him up, and he is taken away afterward.

"What do you think? Have they got hold of Mother?" Pavlusha asks.

"No, Auntie Sonya sent her a telegram. She won't come here."

It is true; Mother took care not to return. When she

received the telegram in Tula with its agreed code word she understood everything. Nor did she bring any cartridges with her. She had good reason to suspect she was being followed. When she boarded the train at Tula to go to Moscow, she noticed the two "fellow travelers" who had accompanied her previously from Moscow. These "fellow travelers" arrested her at a Moscow Station.

Sonya Lepinskaya took us to her place. She already knew about Mother's arrest, and now she had us on her hands. Friends came, among them the Rjevskys, who offered to take Nadya. Sonya discussed the matter with me as if I were already grown up.

"It might be better if Nadya lived with the Rjevskys. They're fond of children."

I could only nod my head in agreement: I knew how hard it was for Sonya to feed these extra mouths. Fedya was taken over by another family. And I moved from one house to another, until Mother was released.

Chapter Eight

Cartridges

Three months after her arrest, Olga Alliluyeva, Anna's mother, was released from prison. She found work as a seamstress in a fashionable dressmaking salon in Moscow, while Sergei, her husband, after a brief spell at Rostov-on-Don where he was placed under stringent police supervision, again went underground. In the autumn of 1905 he reappeared in Baku. Anna and Pavlusha, the two elder Alliluyev children, were sent to the Caucasus: Anna to Tiflis, where she stayed with her beloved grandmother at Didube, and Pavlusha to Baku, where he joined his father. The younger children Nadya and Fedya remained with their mother in Moscow. Anna Alliluyeva continues the narrative.

It is a pity that Pavlusha is not with me. He would have known before me when the events which everyone has been waiting for will take place. He would have been able to explain everything to me. [A. A. refers to the wave of strikes which had broken out with increased violence in the Caucasus.] But Pavlusha is far away, and I have no news of him, nor of Mother, nor of little Fedya and Nadya. I talk to Grandmother about Moscow.

"It's probably cold there again," I say.

And I recall that Mother still has not bought any "valenkis" [felt boots].

"They shouldn't go out into the streets, really they shouldn't," Grandmother says anxiously.

"It's freezing even inside people's houses in Moscow," I reply.

Granny sighs deeply, and I try to comfort her: "Oh, there are some warm places, you may be sure."

I know that shortly before our departure Mother had intended to rent a separate room for herself and the children. Perhaps she found a room in a warm house. It would be interesting to know how things are going in Moscow, whether they are getting ready, or whether things have quietened down. Pavel will be sorry he was not in Didube and did not see us marching under the red banner. Neither the police nor the gendarmerie dared to stop us. Pavel would have been in the front ranks of the column. Kasimir Mankevich and his friends have rifles. I have seen them. Pavel knows how to handle a rifle, and they would probably have given him one.

I hear that rifles will soon be needed. And cartridges also. They bring heavy wrapped-up bundles for Granny to hide in her rooms. These are cartridges.

One must not say a word about such things but must remain silent about everything, also about the fact that Uncle Vanya has arrived. He turns up suddenly one evening, and Granny has only time to gesture in surprise when we throw ourselves on him.

"Quiet," says Uncle Vanya. "One of you had better go and fetch Kasimir."

Kasimir arrives with his friends, and then they all disappear somewhere one by one. The last one to leave is Uncle Vanya. He creeps out into the street in his soft boots. We listen, but everything is quiet. . . .

A few days later Uncle Vanya says to me: "Niura, how would you like to come with me to Baku?"

I could skip with joy!

"I certainly would! When? Soon?"

"We could get her ready in a couple of days," says Xenia, Kasimir Mankevich's wife, in answer to an inquiring look from Uncle Vanya.

Granny shakes her head when I tell her later that evening that I am off to Baku with Uncle Vanya.

"But you haven't even got an overcoat. What are you going to wear?" she asks.

"We will make her a new overcoat," Uncle Vanya reassures her.

On the following day I go with old Auntie Varya to buy material for the overcoat. It is the first time I have had an overcoat made from new, beautiful, fluffy material. I usually wear stuff made from my aunts' cut-down clothes. Auntie Varya is a dressmaker; she makes the overcoat for me. When the coat is fitted on me, I glance into a fragment of broken mirror and think to myself: "In this overcoat, I shall be the best-dressed girl in Didube."

On the day of departure, I get up at dawn. I am too excited to eat anything.

"Eat," Granny tries to coax me. "You won't find food like this on your journey."

I choke on the sweetish greasy *pilaff* and suddenly become alarmed in case Uncle Vanya goes off without me. But Auntie Xenia comes to fetch me. Uncle Vanya is waiting for me at the Mankevichs. We go off, but I am so nervous I do not notice the impression my overcoat makes on the inhabitants of Didube. And Uncle Vanya wears a new suit, in which I have never seen him before. He looks like one of those well-to-do gentlemen who stroll down Golovinsky Prospect.

"Is everything ready? It's time we got going." Vanya comes quite close to me and says: "You're not afraid of anything, are you, Niura?"

I answer quite truthfully: I am not afraid of anything. Xenia takes me into the other room, and Varya pulls out a long white wrapping from under the bed. I take off my overcoat. She winds the wrapping around me a few times and then sews it onto my vest, trying not to prick me with the needle.

"Not too heavy?" she asks. "Is it comfortable? Walk around a bit."

Then she helps me on with the overcoat and, after inspecting me, appears to be satisfied.

"If you ask me, no one will notice anything."

Although there are only the three of us in the room, Xenia whispers to me:

"Don't let anyone touch you, you understand? No one."

I understand. I am wearing a cartridge belt which I am taking to Baku. Father and his friends need these cartridges.

We ride to the station in an open carriage. When the horses pull up, a porter runs up and removes Vanya's suitcase. Uncle Vanya takes me by the hand and we walk onto the platform. The porter walks behind. I look around the carriage in amazement! How opulent everything looks! There are soft seats, a carpet on the floor and mirrors. This is a second-class carriage, and we usually travel in dirty, bare third-class carriages.

"In here," says the porter, placing the suitcase in a compartment occupied by two officers.

I look at Uncle Vanya, but he takes his time as he settles on the striped seat, inviting me to sit down beside him. As the train begins to move, one of the officers remarks: "We seem to have pleasant company." He picks up a box of sweets from a table and holds it out to me. "Won't you try one of these, miss, please?"

I edge closer to Uncle Vanya: he smiles and says: "We are not very fond of sweets, I think. . . ."

"No, I insist, the young lady must try one."

"Well, since you have been asked, you can hardly refuse the invitation," says Vanya.

I take a chocolate from the box. Afterward I go into the

train corridor and look out at the mountains which we pass. Uncle Vanya talks with the officers.

"May I be so bold as to ask if you are going to Baku?" they inquire.

"Yes," Uncle Vanya replies.

"The devil only knows what's going on there," the officer who offered me the sweets says. "People are really getting out of hand."

"You are quite right, sir," Uncle Vanya replies as usual in his quiet, even voice.

The conductor comes and lights an oil lamp in the compartment when it grows dark. Vanya calls me and says it is time for me to go to sleep. I want to take off my overcoat, and one of the officers stretches out a hand to help me. But Uncle Vanya smiles politely, removes my coat and lifts me up to the top bunk. I lie on the bunk feeling the cartridge belt which is wound around me, and I shiver apprehensively: what would have happened if the officer had discovered the cartridges! It is not very comfortable to lie there, but I dare not move. Soon I am fast asleep and when I open my eyes the train is drawing up at Baku.

"We've arrived," says Uncle Vanya.

He helps me down from the bunk, assists me with my coat, and we walk out onto the platform.

In the room to which we are subsequently taken, an unknown woman undresses me and removes the cartridges. She hugs me to her and says; "You're a wonderful little girl!"

When I recounted the story about the cartridges to Mother some months later, the story had a somewhat different ending.

"Weren't they a little too heavy for you?" Mother asked, anxiously.

"No," I said, showing my independence. "I walked round Baku for a whole day with them."

And I was instantly shocked at my own lie.

Mother complained to Uncle Vanya because he had not removed the cartridges immediately.

"What do you think, Olga, of course we took them off her straight away."

I heard what was said in the other room and nearly burst into tears with shame. But Uncle Vanya seemed to sense something. He said; "If it had been necessary she would have walked around with them a couple of days or so. That's why she felt as if she had done so."

Chapter Nine

Massacres

It is possible that after my journey with the cartridges, there was no one to take me back to Granny in Tiflis, or that Father simply did not want to part with me, but I can see myself back at the house in the electric power station in Baku where we all lived together four years before. Here is the upstairs room where I probably first saw Nadya in swaddling clothes. The house was still under construction at that time, but now it has been renovated. The balconies which were being built now have railings. Now Mother would not be afraid that we would fall off. I remember there was a dreadful fright when Pavlusha was discovered hanging from one of these unfinished balconies. Mother was beside herself as she dragged him back into the room.

And here is the same seashore where we used to skip from one rock to another. And a little farther off, behind the house, is the quay where boats were moored. How happy we were when Mother took us for a walk and we would stop near the big hawsers wrapped in thick mooring ropes and watch swarthy, noisy little boys splashing about or diving into the waters of the quay.

I recall this quay particularly clearly because it was here that Father was almost drowned. Even now I can recall the somewhat comic episode which almost finished in tragedy, since it involved our overzealous and determined father.

We were walking along the quay when the wind suddenly carried away my new straw hat, which floated out to sea. I had barely had time to cry out when Father threw off his jacket and trousers, dived into the water and swam off after the hat. But it refused to be captured so easily and continued to drift farther and farther out to sea. Horror-stricken at this unexpected turn of events, we stood frozen at the quayside.

"Sergei, what are you doing? Come back!" Mother's cry was carried away by the wind.

As usual the treacherous Baku north wind came up suddenly. The waves rose higher, carrying the straw hat on their crest, tormenting us with anxiety. Father was a fast, skillful swimmer, but he could not grab the hat.

"Come back, come back, Father!" we cried, running up and down the quay.

But Father did not hear us and continued obstinately to chase after the light straw ring which was rapidly disappearing from our view.

We had never seen the sea so menacing and shouted all the louder. But a moment or two later we were laughing through our tears, as Father approached with the hat stuck proudly on his head, its band fluttering bravely near his beard.

But now at this moment I am by myself, without Mother and Pavlusha, in a small room on the ground floor of the house at the power station. My father sleeps on a narrow little iron bed and I make myself comfortable every evening on top of a large trunk. Georgi Rtvelazde's wife Natasha, the one who took the cartridges off me, brought me here. A gray-eyed woman met us at the house.

"My name is Dunya," she said.

Afterward everything became clear to me. Father and I were living in the apartment of his old friend Nazarov.

Uncle Vanya also visits the Nazarovs. Every Sunday he takes me for a walk and buys me Caucasian sweetmeats, such as heads of sweetcorn sprinkled with sugar. The Tartar [Turkish] hawkers prepare them on charcoal burners which they carry around with them in the streets.

Everything seems to take place in the streets. They shave and cut hair in the street. I stop Uncle Vanya so as to watch these street barbers at work. Men get up from low benches and put their greasy, dirty caps on the shaven crowns of their heads. These are porters, the *ambals* as they are called in Baku. I follow them as they walk in the middle of the street, bent and shaking beneath excessive loads. They sleep right on the pavements, in the dust, with their bearer's rings of coiled rope tucked under their heads. This rather surprises me.

"Why do they sleep out here and not in their homes?" I ask Uncle Vanya.

"And how do you know if they have any homes?" he asks. "They've probably nowhere else to sleep since they sleep in the street. . . ."

The poor creatures, I think to myself. Why doesn't anyone help them? Why do well-dressed people go by without noticing these porters who lie in the dusty streets?

Dignified, red-bearded Moslems swagger by without deigning to look at anyone. Behind them, on clattering heels, glide strange figures in whispering silks. Between the slits in their silken masks glow fiery black eyes. I follow them with a mixture of fear and curiosity. "These are Moslem wives with their husband," someone remarks.

"Wives! Just like Bluebeard's!" I say to myself.

And this little thing, hardly bigger than myself, is she also a wife? I am sorely tempted to pull away the yellow kerchief from this comic little figurine of a wife and see what is hidden behind the bright-colored silk. Is it an ordinary human face? And then in a flash, as if in answer to my thought, or so it appeared to me, she drew a piece of vivid cloth across her face.

"Uncle Vanya!" I shouted, triumphantly, "Uncle Vanya, but she's only a girl!"

But while Anna Alliluyeva's impressionable years were filled with the exotic customs of the Moslem inhabitants of Baku, a savage clash occurred between the Christian Armenians and their Turkish neighbors, encouraged by the ultranationalist "Black Hundreds" and the "Russian People's Union." Their object was to divert the popular clamor for reforms and stem the tide of revolution, as Isaac Deutscher has pointed out:

"What the Jews were in other parts of the Empire, the scapegoats on whom Tzardom tried to divert popular discontent, the Armenians were in the Caucasus."[16] Sergei Alliluyev gives an account of one such massacre by the Turkish population directed against the Armenians following a strike among oil workers in Baku.

To begin with, the gangs [Black Hundreds] began to foment clashes between Armenian and Turkish children. The children wounded each other, and because of this fierce quarrels broke out among their elders. The Black Hundred gangs lay in wait for Turks and Armenians, slaying them and burning their homes. Fanning national hatreds between them, the authorities achieved their ends through artificial means. In August the Armenians and Turks began wholesale slaughter.

The town echoed with shots: Armenian shops were looted and homes were attacked. Corpses were flung onto streets and pavements. The wounded moaned in this bloodshed. In some places soldiers and policemen were to be seen standing around watching the massacre without raising a hand.

The Black Hundreds, encouraged by the authorities, began setting fire to factories and oil derricks, spreading wild rumors that these acts had been perpetrated by strikers. Pretending to "fight against arsonists," the bandits and assassins hunted out many of our leading party workers.

The Baku section of the Russian Social Democratic Party found it necessary to summon all the workers of the town to a general strike. Everyday life came to an end.

Existence became a living hell. The fires at the oil refineries grew more and more threatening. We were caught up in some terrifying, overwhelming and unquenchable holocaust. Death and destruction surrounded us.

A number of Armenian families, together with their children, sought shelter at the electricity power station to save themselves from the pogrom organizers. . . .

Anna Alliluyeva recalls one such episode when her father went out of his way to rescue victims of the massacres.

I sit quietly in the corner of Dunya Nazarov's little room. I should probably be in bed, but everyone has forgotten about me. Suddenly there is a commotion outside the house.

"Fire! Fire! The oil refineries are alight!" come shouts from the corridor.

Father and Vanya Nazarov and other workers at the power station run into the room. I have never seen Father look so angry.

"I'll not allow it!" he exclaims, striking his fist on the table. "These cowards are only looking after their own interests! I shall go and open the doors myself. Don't they understand—children are involved!"

"But we've children of our own!" someone present says. "What if they were to break in and kill our children?"

"Let's go," Father says firmly and harshly. "I shall open the doors myself."

I grasped the situation. A crowd of Armenians, mothers and children, had come to the gates of the power station, clamoring to be saved.

There was more noise in the corridor, followed by timid footsteps. I could hear Dunya's voice: "This way, this way," she was saying.

A group of women enter, their clothes in tatters, holding children in their arms. An older boy clings to his mother's skirts.

"Please sit down," Dunya invites them.

But the women continue to stand. They hesitate to sit on the snow-white bedspreads. Finally they settle down, petrified, crestfallen, frozen into immobility. Then the little boy falls on his knees before his mother, whimpering and then bursting into sobs. The women try to calm the child, and then interrupting each other, explain in broken Russian: "They burned everything, everything! Everyone was killed. . . ."

Neither Father nor Vanya Nazarov sleeps that night. I hear their footsteps in the corridor and I lie very still on top of my trunk where I have my bed. Now I can relax: the women and children who are sleeping in Dunya's room have someone to defend them.

I am not allowed out of the house, but in the morning I manage to slip out from under Dunya's observant eye. I race into the yard with our neighbor's children. We climb up the fire escape and watch the conflagration from the roof. The wind is fanning the smoky flames of the Bibi-Eybat refineries. Before our elders can reach us and shoo us away, we go and stand in front of the heavily barred gates of the power station. These are rarely opened now, because it is dangerous to go outside the confines of the station. Shooting, murder and arson continue in the city.

When Father and Vanya Nazorov sit down to drink tea in the evening, Dunya says, with a preoccupied gesture: "There's no more bread in the power station. How shall I feed the children tomorrow? I must go into town to find food."

"I've spoken to the driver, but he's frightened to take his carriage into town," Vanya Nazarov says, frowning more than usual. But Father interrupts him: "We'll talk him into going. We'll all go, together with Dunya. Are you willing, Dunya?"

"Of course, I'll go," Dunya says solemnly.

Next morning the sullen coachman drives the horse-omnibus to our house. Father and Dunya get in with a large wicker basket which they push under their knees, and the omnibus leaves for town.

When they return, I hear the driver complaining angrily to all and sundry: "I won't do that journey again, not for all the money in the world! Life's too precious! It's lucky we got out alive. Why, they killed a man right in front of your eyes. . . ."

. . . Other events grow confused in my memory, but one day Father disappeared. All the grown-ups became disturbed and there was a heavy, oppressive silence in all the rooms. Only a short while before that, I heard the stamp of heavy boots out in the yard, and the sound of rifle bolts being drawn, and someone came rushing into the room, to announce: "The troops are here! They've surrounded the power station. . . ."

Next morning Dunya talked gently to me as she helped me to dress.

"Where's Father?" I asked.

Dunya did not answer immediately.

"We'll go and find him, very soon perhaps we'll be able to see him."

"But where is he?"

I looked up hopelessly at her, but Dunya only turned away.

A few days later I saw Father standing in the yard of a long stone building; on either side of him were policemen with lifted rifles. I was not allowed to go near Father. Dunya held my hand firmly.

"Goodbye!" Father called out. "Remember me to Granny. . . ."

Chapter Ten

Kars: a Scene from Gogol

Sergei Alliluyev was released from prison and returned to Baku, but following a general strike he was arrested again, together with some thirty other persons. In September 1905 the prisoners were taken to Kars, a fortress town situated on the border of Turkey.

Having arrived in Kars, we were put into five small cells on the ground floor of the new provincial prison. A corridor led to a smallish yard, surrounded by a high stone wall. Two of the smallest cells were allotted to the women prisoners. Once the guards had brought us in, the prison governor began the roll call.

"There are thirty-two of us; here is the list of names. That can do in place of a roll call," I said, as leader of our group.

The governor looked up uncomprehendingly.

"Where do you think you are—in jail or in a hotel?" he asked. "The prison has its own regulations and you are expected to obey them."

"Exactly," I answered. "But we gave no undertaking of any sort before we left Baku."

The prison governor, a Greek with a large nose and extremely small eyes, became angry.

"There's really no need to get angry, Mr. Governor," Lefass [another prisoner] said mockingly. "Keep calm. You've probably got a wife and children, and you seem a pleasant sort of chap. But you won't get a thing out of us. We told you there's no need for roll calls and we mean what we say. We're a pretty determined lot."

The warders exchanged glances and shrugged their shoulders. The governor gave up, too. Our belongings were searched and we were asked to hand over our personal articles and money, for which we were handed receipts.

The next day the local authorities paid us a visit. Among them were the head of the gendarmerie, the chief police inspector and other bigwigs. After a brief exchange of pleasantries, they inspected our cells and concluded that we were quite comfortable. We were not prepared to argue: the cells were indeed quite cozy and clean. They bowed politely and were about to leave when we stopped them.

"We're reasonably satisfied with our cells, but we have a number of requests to make nevertheless," we said.

"Requests?" the police inspector echoed.

"Yes, requests," we repeated.

"Surely you mean petitions?" the inspector prompted kindly.

"No, not petitions," I said. "Petitions you might not grant, but requests . . ."

"And how do you think we would respond to . . . requests?" the inspector asked expectantly.

"Requests you would have to grant," Lefass said firmly. To cut short this exchange, the authorities said they would listen to our requests. We demanded that oil lamps should replace the small wick lamps and that women prisoners should be given a separate washstand from the men. We also asked that our prison pay should be increased from twelve to twenty kopecks.

The astonished representatives of law and order pointed

out that we were obviously not familiar with the rules and regulations governing prison administration. We on our part felt bound to tell the public prosecutor and other leading citizens that we were well acquainted with the interior of Russian prisons, and that we had struggled to change the existing order and more specifically the regulations governing prisons.

Two or three days later all our requests were granted. We succeeded in annoying the prison warders, however, by singing revolutionary songs in unison every day. The town authorities were thoroughly scared of the revolutionary movement in the country and had to tolerate this kind of behavior whether they liked it or not.

On October 18 [1905], the same town representatives turned up shortly after lunch and announced that following the Tzar's published Manifesto of the previous day, we were to be released, our sentences remitted and a full pardon given to us. Instead of thanking them, we shouted in one voice: "Long live the Revolution! Down with tyranny!"

Freed from jail through the expression of popular power, we made our way into the town. Here we divided into groups in order to measure public feeling. The town of Kars itself was an impressive fortress, with numerous soldiers and a horde of civil servants, civilian and military.

Great excitement prevailed and the town was crowded. Everyone appeared to be under the spell of the Manifesto of October 17.[17] We used this mood of general elation to hold a meeting of our own. Many people gathered, and we made speeches against the Tzar and the existing order.

When darkness fell, we had to think of a place to lodge. Since all our belongings were still in the prison, we decided to return to our cells and spend the night there. When we knocked at the prison gates, the governor himself came out to meet us.

"What can I do for you, gentlemen?" he asked, smiling.

As group leader I explained that we had come to collect

our things but asked whether he would be hospitable enough to allow us to sleep in the prison of which he was in charge. The governor appeared to be so flattered that he threw caution to the winds and forgot all about prison regulations.

"Of course, gentlemen, you are welcome to return to your cells," he said, still smiling. And so we returned to "our" cells. . . .

While we were resting in our cells, the town authorities heard all about the public meeting which we had organized. They wanted to know where we would be spending the night. The entire police force, including the chief of police and the inspector, turned out to look for us. They searched all the corners of the town but to no avail. Finally they stumbled on the man who had served us supper. He told them that we had returned to prison to collect our belongings.

The authorities were furious. At about nine in the evening the prison governor visited our cell, his hair disheveled, and began moaning that we had taken him for a simpleton, and that he would now be charged with allowing unauthorized persons into the prison. He urged us to leave. The chief of police arrived shortly afterward.

"Clear out of here immediately," he ordered.

We replied that as we could not get satisfactory lodgings in town, we would have to stay in prison until morning. The chief of police countered by suggesting that we should remove ourselves to a barracks built as an emergency hospital in the event of outbreaks of cholera. But we categorically turned down this honor, saying that we were tired and should like to be left alone. He gave way, and we fell fast asleep.

On the following morning we again left the prison without taking our belongings. We were told that leaflets had appeared during the night in the garrison barracks, printed in Russian and Armenian. These leaflets had, in fact, been printed by a group of our comrades who had stayed the night in town for that purpose.

We split into several small groups, after agreeing to meet in the town park at a given hour. We then went to workshops, cafés and teahouses to talk to craftsmen, the intelligentsia, students, and especially to soldiers belonging to the local garrison. Talking to soldiers, we heard of the conflicts which had arisen between lower ranks and officers in certain military formations.

An enormous crowd had gathered at the park for our public meeting. Among them were soldiers, students, officers, as well as various departmental civil servants who had come with their wives and relatives. The meeting opened with a speech from a representative of the local intelligentsia. Following him came speeches from our comrades, warning their listeners not to have any illusions about the newly given freedoms. They also attacked the military caste who had played such an inglorious and treacherous role during the Russo-Japanese war, subjecting millions of Russian soldiers to unheard-of suffering and deprivation. These speeches received an enthusiastic and warm welcome from a majority of the audience. But many of the officers and higher civil servants, who resented these attacks, left the meeting. We brought the proceedings to a close by reminding the soldiers and students to come to the park on the following day at the same hour for another public meeting.

On October 20 mounted patrols appeared in the town. Despite this, a large crowd gathered in the park.

Lefass and the local provincial governor could be observed walking side by side in the park. The governor of the province of Kars was trying to persuade Lefass to influence his friends to be more careful in their speeches.

"The Manifesto was not issued so as to enable anyone to use strong language against the Tzar's family," he said, looking appealingly at Lefass. "Now, isn't that so?"

He complained that the military commander of the

Kars fortress was putting pressure on him, demanding that firm and definite measures should be taken against us.

"As head of the province, I fully appreciate the commander's concern for his fortress and garrison. But what am I expected to do when I haven't received any instructions from the center? All that I have received is this Manifesto, granting certain freedoms." The provincial governor took Lefass by the arm. "How can I take repressive measures?"

"Naturally you can't," Lefass exclaimed, surprised. "The Manifesto forbids such measures."

"What am I to do, then?" The governor's voice trembled. "It's a dreadful situation."

"It certainly is, Your Excellency. It could hardly be worse. If you oppose the higher authorities, you'll be in trouble. And if you go against the revolutionaries you might end up hanging from the nearest pole. Who knows?"

The governor shuddered and sighed: "Indeed, these are difficult times." He then added sadly, "It's just my luck that I should have a problem like this on my hands. And at my age, too! It's all thanks to Fadeyev, the governor of Baku. As if he couldn't find any other province for exiled revolutionaries! It had to be my town—Kars—and no other!"

While the Provincial Governor was appealing to Lefass to moderate his language, an armed detachment, with an officer at its head, came down the stone steps leading into the park and moved quickly in the direction of the public meeting. Lefass, who noticed the soldiers, asked the governor: "What's the meaning of this?"

The governor shrugged his shoulders helplessly.

"What can I do? It's nothing to do with me." And bowing elegantly to Lefass, he disappeared.

As the soldiers approached, people became agitated. We appealed to them to hold their ground and not to panic.

The officer in charge came up and began swearing at us like a coachman.

"Round them up, and if they resist use your bayonets," he ordered his men.

A murmur of protest rose from the crowd. The soldiers stood quite still, their faces dead white. One after another, they lowered their rifles.

"Surround them!" the officer repeated, swinging his bared sword.

The soldiers continued to stand motionless, gazing at the crowd who now began to express out loud their disapproval of the officer's behavior.

At that moment another detachment of soldiers appeared. We again appealed to the public to keep calm so as to avoid a clash and prevent bloodshed. We then turned to the soldiers and told them that if they thought it necessary to obey their superior's orders, they should make a circle and we would step into it voluntarily. The soldiers' faces brightened at this solution, and they willingly formed a circle, which we entered.

We then invited the chief of police and the prosecutor to explain the presence of armed soldiers. The prosecutor explained that while the new constitution allowed public meetings, the persons responsible were asked to give details of place, date and hour of such meetings.

"You have already held three such meetings without reference to the town authorities," he continued. "You are therefore under arrest and are duly sentenced to two days' imprisonment."

Loud disapproval and anger greeted these words. Local Armenian youths who supported us offered to put up a fight to prevent our arrest. But we declined their offer and made a move toward our hospitable prison where we were to sit it out for a couple of days.

The young men, however, insisted on following us, running behind our escort, whistling and heckling the officer who strode at the head of his men. We could see that he was blushing from embarrassment. When we crossed the street where the provincial governor lived, he suddenly jumped into a cab and disappeared, followed by hoots and yells from the crowd.

According to Sergei Alliluyev this officer, "a detestable, unpleasant German," tried to rally the soldiers of the garrison to disperse the crowds, but having failed to find a reliable body of men, got into a furious temper and died from a heart attack. Meanwhile Alliluyev and thirty-one of his friends, now back in prison for their two-day sentence, determined to make the lives of the mild prison governor and his staff as miserable as possible. They succeeded amply.

Back in jail, we again caused trouble and annoyance to the administration. When they counted us, they discovered that our group now consisted of some sixty persons, although they held warrants for the arrest of only thirty-two. The chief of police and the public prosecutor tried to explain to the superfluous number of young men who had followed us to prison that only those who had been sent from Baku were arrested, the others were free to leave. The young men insisted that since they had initiated the public meeting they should now share the fate of their comrades. The dilemma for the chief of police and the prosecutor was excruciating. They proposed that a roll call should be held so as to establish the real prisoners' identities. But this maneuver fell through: we all kept silent. The prison governor then offered to identify us by remembering our faces. He began by pointing me out. I told him to drop this nonsense. He gave up, mumbling that he knew no one and knew nothing, and left. The matter ended with our being returned to the cells we had occupied the previous day.

On October 23 our two-day prison sentence came to an end. We told our friends who had supplied us with food that we would be freed at five that afternoon, and that we would therefore not be eating supper in jail. We asked them to prepare a meal for us in town.

We anticipated that normal rail services between Kars and Tiflis, which had been interrupted by a strike, would be restarted on either the 23rd or 24th. We planned to leave by the first train. But at about one o'clock in the afternoon, the chief of police arrived at the prison and announced that we should be released at eleven that evening. We protested and demanded to be released at five, otherwise we reserved the right to take appropriate action.

The chief of police went off to report to the prison governor and the prosecutor. He returned at three and told us that much as he regretted it it was impossible to grant our request as this would undermine the prestige of the authorities. We, on our part, refused to make any concessions since our request appeared to be reasonable and again insisted on being set free at five o'clock.

"We will wait until four-fifty at the latest," I told the chief of police.

He shrugged his shoulders, saluted and left.

Some of us were prepared to accept the situation and remain in prison until the following morning. I wanted to obstruct the authorities and the majority supported me. Someone pointed out that we had no moral right to put our young friends who had joined us in prison into jeopardy. We decided to give these youngsters a chance to make up their minds. Ten minutes later they said they would support any action we might take.

The group of prisoners from Baku then plotted a plan of action. We would break all the windows in the cells, destroy the plank beds and doors.

At precisely ten to five I clapped my hands and there arose a tremendous noise of breaking glass, shattered wood and stones. Clouds of pungent dust filled the place.

A few minutes later the prison was surrounded by soldiers, but by this time we had completed our job. We sat down to drink tea in the communal cell, waiting for the outcome.

As always, after great excitement came the reaction: we became depressed. The minutes ticked away painfully. Somewhere an unbolted door creaked. I rose, approached the door and looked cautiously into the corridor. Tense silence everywhere. I felt awful. My knees shook with apprehension: I was afraid of the deathly silence. But suddenly, at the end of the corridor a head appeared, then another, followed by a third, all with pale, distracted faces. These belonged to members of the local authority. When I saw how lost they looked, I felt better and went into the corridor to offer them the hospitality of our cell. My friends who saw me making ceremonious bows toward someone became very excited. A group of civil servants appeared at our door. The chief clerk of the gubernatorial office said, in a quivering voice, that His Excellency the governor of the province had graciously consented to our immediate release.

We were soon trooping by the prison office at whose door stood the provincial governor and his staff. They followed our progress with hostile eyes. Lefass smiled as he passed the governor.

"*Au revoir,* Your Excellency. Thanks for the pleasant conversation."

"Goodbye," the governor answered softly and weakly. "Goodbye," he repeated in a somewhat sterner voice.

The last to leave the prison was Bakradze. He came up to one of the prison guards, slapped him on the back, and said: "As you see, comrade, you had nothing to worry about. It all turned out happily."

The sentry snapped to a salute and shouted: "At your command! Just as you said!"

Our journey from Kars to Tiflis resembled a demonstration. We had a red satin flag embroidered in multicolored silks, which had been sewn by some Armenian women in Kars. Whenever we approached a station, we hung the flag out of the carriage window, and our choir, led by the young irrepressible Bolshevik "Solomonchik," Pavel Bliakhin, would begin singing revolutionary songs. People who gathered at the station cheered us loudly.

Sergei Alliluyev went to live at Nakhalovka, a working-class suburb of Tiflis, while Anna Alliluyeva remained with her grandmother in Didube. She returns to her narrative.

Chapter Eleven

Riot

There is a hum of feverish activity in the field in front of the workshops. Armed workers patrol the streets. They belong to the popular militia, as we now call them. Their ranks have been swollen by new friends who appear on the outskirts of Tiflis on their short, lean little horses. We always stopped to admire these skilled horsemen in their cowls, enormous sheepskin coats and soft, high leather boots. They are peasants and shepherds who have come down from the hills to join in the struggle by the workers' side. Detachments of these hill men are gathering at Nakhalovka and Didube.

So far not a shot has been heard, but Granny has locked my young aunts and myself in our rooms.

"This is no time for children to go gadding about the streets," she says.

That is easier said than done. We will find some way of creeping outside unnoticed. Suddenly the morning silence is broken by the sharp harsh bark of a rifle, followed by fusillades. We run to the windows and watch the militiamen scurrying down the streets as the firing continues. The shots seem to be far away, but our women neighbors bring urgent news to Granny.

"Troops are moving toward Didube and Nakhalovka. The militia are preparing their defense."

"Our chaps have barricaded themselves in the Big House." The Big House was a stone three-storied building not far from us.

The shooting continues into the night. We cannot sleep as we listen to the shots reverberating in the hills. By morning troops have broken into Didube and Cossack horses flash by our windows.

"They are on their way to Nakhalovka to search for arms," gossip in the yard informs us. But it is useless for the women to try to get out into the street. It is ringed with Cossacks and policemen, and the Cossacks wave everyone back to their houses with their whips. More rifle shots follow, but now they are quite deafening. Someone says the Big House is surrounded by Cossacks but that the militiamen refuse to surrender.

Granny pushes us away from the window, but we have managed to get a glimpse of a gun lumbering down the street. It is positioned outside the Big House.

The scenes which I witnessed from the window of my grandmother's little house were part of the spirit of resistance which arose in Russia during the First Revolution. The summons to arms made by the Bolsheviks was enthusiastically answered by the peasant hill men who had been secretly armed and recruited by Tiflis workers. Their job was to filter into Tiflis to prepare convenient strong points strategically placed in the city. But the cowardly Menshevik traitors demanded that the partisan forces should be concentrated in the working-class settlements of Didube and Nakhalovka.

The Bolsheviks knew that it was pointless to start an uprising in the closely built-up area of the working-class districts, since the authorities would move their troops into those districts before a single shot had been fired. It was imperative to concentrate one's forces in districts partially occupied by workers, such as Kuki, Avlabar, Peski, Ortachali and the Moslem quarter, with the object of drawing sympathizers into the combat and seizing the most vital points in the city such as the railway station, the post office and the banks. This Bolshevik plan of action was warmly supported by the hill men, who were prepared to fight in their own craggy hilltop villages as well as in their native hills where every rock and bush would afford them shelter.

The partisans were ready to answer the call from the Bolsheviks and to settle accounts with the Tzarist authorities. They were also prepared to take over the streets in the city and to leave the outskirts of Nakhalovka and Didube where the Mensheviks tried to lure them. But the Mensheviks cunningly and persistently opposed the Bolshevik plan of action and finally managed to persuade the hill men to abandon the city.

The enemy also had his problems. The authorities decided to disarm their less reliable troops. Soldiers were confined to barracks and all leave was cancelled. News came from the barracks that the authorities were preparing a devastating attack on Didube and Nakhalovka. Workers' squads armed with revolvers and bombs [probably homemade explosives] were ready at their posts to repulse the attack.

Mankevich's house in Nakhalovka where Father lived stood behind some railway lines, close to the barracks which housed the military sappers, the most revolutionary-minded part of Tiflis. A few days before the sappers had been disarmed. But one night Father and Kasimir Mankevich were told that orders had been given for the advance on the settlements, and infantry, cavalry and artillery were to move out in full battle order and preparation.

No one slept that night. People watched from the windows as cavalry rode purposefully through the streets, followed by the rattle of the artillery train and behind them the ambulance carts. At dawn rifle shots could be heard which seemed to come from the hills. The firing continued without interruption. Father left the house with Kasimir and met a detachment of infantry. They were convoying a couple of arrested men, one of whom Father recognized immediately as "Vanechka," an Armenian militiaman from Nakhalovka, a splendid trophy for the police to have picked up.

The other prisoner walked with a coat flung over his head. He pulled back the coat to reveal the thick, dry crusted blood on his face and looked at Father.

"Kamo!" Father could barely restrain himself.

Yes, it was Kamo. The police had seized one of the most courageous and most beloved of Stalin's young pupils.[18]

Soldiers were much in evidence that night in the settlements, bursting into people's rooms and courtyards looking for arms. But everyone had been warned and the arms had been hidden.

Under pressure from regular forces, the guerrillas refused open combat; they retreated into the interior of the settlement toward a gorge, hoping to make their way into the hills. The military had anticipated this maneuver and had sent Cossack scouts to cut off the partisan retreat from the rear. The partisans stumbled on them on the road to the Salt Lake, by the Hudatovsky wood. The scouts crawled on the ground and took aim with their rifles. The ambush had succeeded and the partisans had no alternative except to open fire and try to break through the ring.

. . . When the revolutionary staff met, shortly after the departure of the troops, they were interrupted by the arrival of a forester from the Hudatovsky wood.

"Hurry up!" he shouted breathlessly from the threshold. "The woods are filled with dead men. But there's one living. . . ."

He turned on his heel and began to run back from where he came. Father and his friends ran after him. On the way, the forester told them that the corpses strewn over the hillside were riddled with bullets and pierced with bayonets.[19] A wounded man had managed to crawl to his hut and had told him, before losing consciousness, to fetch his friends and to tell them that the partisans had not died like cowards but had refused to surrender or to ask for mercy, and had fought to the bitter end, facing the foe.

The wounded man was picked up and bandaged. He had received twelve bayonet wounds, but he was still alive. They managed to save his life.

The dead were removed to one of the houses in the settlement and people came to bid farewell to the heroes. The funeral rites lasted for a long time and a communal grave was dug on the side of the hill behind the settlement where they fell, surrendering their lives for their Revolution.

A mournful silence hangs over Didube and Nakhalovka. Since the soldiers have left, we can venture out into the streets, and a terrible vision of death and destruction meets our eyes. We pass in silence; we know that "they" have won. But is this really the end? We stand in front of the Big House. It is in ruins because a field gun destroyed the top story, and below, in place of windows, there are gaps. But our friends who occupied the house had not surrendered but had managed to escape. I know, I am certain, that they are safe and will return to fight another day.

Now everyone goes to Nakhalovka. They move slowly and stop in front of the house where Father lives. He comes out and I rush up to him.

"So you're also here, Niura! Well, see you attend to your schoolwork," he tells me.

The dead are laid out on biers, washed and prepared for burial.

"They were killed," Shura [one of Anna Alliluyeva's young aunts] whispers. But a man who stands next to us presses his fist into the palm of his hand and says loudly: "They'll pay dearly for them. . . ."

As we leave the house, a bitter thought enters my head: The end is not yet in sight. I will, I want to carry cartridges, illegal leaflets, if only to avenge the deaths of our good comrades.

Chapter Twelve

Reunion

Shortly afterward Father came to fetch me at Grandmother's house.

"Get ready," he said; "we are going to Baku."

Once more I have to bid Granny goodbye and part with my young aunts and my friends. Father notices my sorrow and begins to tease me.

"You've quite forgotten about your mother," he says, reproachfully. "She's also coming to Baku . . ."

I cannot find words to express myself. So much has happened recently since we all lived together and Mother had charge of us and Pavlusha and I played together, sharing our joys and sorrows.

"Are they all coming? Pavlusha also?" I ask as my voice returns to me.

"All of them," Father replies. "It's time we were all together," he adds to himself.

Granny sighs heavily as she packs my few scanty belongings and Father and I leave.

Mother, Pavlusha, Fedya and Nadya arrive at the house on the Bailov peninsula where Father has found us an apartment. It is in the basement and the windows look out onto the street. A stone yard slopes down to the sea. I am glad that the sea is so near.

So at last the family is together again. Goodness, how Fedya and Nadya have grown! We discuss events in Moscow around the table. Mother sometimes forgets or omits some detail and Pavlusha and Fedya prompt her.

Mother was living in a room on the Bronaya when the rising took place in the Presna district.[19] She had packed Pavlusha off to Nizhni Novgorod to Sonya Lepinskaya, but took a room for herself in the wooden house belonging to a carter. In this hole there was barely room to put a bed. She brought Fedya with her, but Nadya went to stay with the Rjevskys.

"I was working all day at the dressmaking shop," Mother explains. "It was terrible to leave Fedya all by himself."

"It wasn't at all terrible. I wasn't at all frightened," says Fedya.

Fedya describes the strikes in Moscow. Water supplies stopped functioning and people had to resort to wells. Pavlusha explains that there were only a few dozen wells in Moscow and that these were stone dry within a very few days.

"We had our own well in the yard," Fedya interjects, hurriedly. "You can't imagine the crowds who came to use it."

I cannot get used to the fact that Fedya has matured and is now a person in his own right. And Mother, who grasps my incredulity, observes: "Don't pull Fedya's leg. He fought on the barricades." She takes pride in talking about her youngest son.

On the evening of December 9 [1905] when she was returning home from work there was firing in the streets. It took her some hours to cross from the Strasny Boulevard to Bronaya. It was already dark when she approached her house. She noticed that a barricade was being constructed: barrels were being rolled up and people were throwing tables and chairs from their windows to build up the barricade. A young lad climbed to the top.

Mother stopped. She recognized Fedya standing on the barricade, holding tightly to one of the striker's hands.

"Afterward I went to fetch Nadya," Mother says, continuing her account. "Again there was firing in the streets. It was dangerous to be out, but we got to the house all right."

Fedya hurries to add: "As soon as Mother and Nadya left, a bomb exploded in the Rjevskys' house."

Pavlusha tells an equally interesting story. He always seems to know about things which I have not discovered for myself. I also hear the word *Potemkin*[20] from Pavlusha for the first time.

"The cruiser *Potemkin* was the ship which mutinied against the Tzar. It steamed out to sea although it was menaced by the guns."

I get this rather hazy account from Pavlusha about the ship which first raised the banner of revolt.

"I'll let you into a secret," Pavlusha whispers conspiratorially. "Uncle Vanya hid sailors from the *Potemkin*."

"From the *Potemkin?*"

"Yes, of course, from the cruiser *Potemkin*."

It appears that two sailors from the *Potemkin* were making their way through Baku. Father's job was to hide the two men and he brought them to Uncle Vanya. The sailors hid for a few days in Vanya's room and then managed to slip away.

Pavlusha also saw armed workers patroling the streets in Nizhni.

"They were demanding their rights," he says. "After all, as you know, everything should belong to them by right. But the bosses sent out police and gendarmes. They had more weapons and were able to bring up artillery. That's why they won.

"But one day the workers will also have heavy guns! You'll see!"

And we suddenly remember our friend Sasha Nikiforov whom the gendarmes have hanged. It is an unbearable thought; we shudder and grow silent.

We can enjoy the sea and the sun to our heart's content in Baku. A small pier juts out from our sloping yard into the sea. Pavlusha has developed a new hobby; he is learning to fish. He sits motionless on the pier, holding his fishing tackle and dangling his feet in the water. A cluster of tiny, silver-blue fish hang around his hook and string: no other fish rise to his bait.

Because today is Sunday, Mother has dressed Nadya and me in our best white dresses. But where else can we go except to the pier where Pavlusha is busy fishing? Holding hands, we go up to him. The fish glitter in the sun on his hook. I bend down to touch him. Suddenly there is a cry behind me which grows into a wail. Nadya! I had let go of her hand and she had slipped off the edge of a rickety plank and had fallen straight into the oily water. Before I had time to cry out, Pavlusha was already under the pier. He comes out holding Nadya, wrings the water from her dress and places her down beside me. The dress is ruined, but no harm has come to Nadya; she is already laughing. It will not be easy to hide this little adventure from Mother. I pick Nadya up and take her home.

Our peaceful life at Bailov beside the sea does not last long. We can sense that something is brewing. Father returns home scowling. Our elders, who gather at our place in the evening, ignore us. They discuss their own affairs and normal life is interrupted. Father does not go out to work and from early morning people turn up at our apartment.

"There's a strike at the electricity power station," Pavlusha says. "Father is on the strike committee."

The strike comes to an end and Pavlusha is the first to discover this. What is going to happen now? New troubles are upon us. We run down to the sea where the waves lap just as if nothing has happened. But we have come to say goodbye to the waves. Mother has started to pack and we must help her, for tomorrow we leave for Tiflis.

Chapter Thirteen

Brief Respite

Didube greets us like birds of passage who have circled over unfamiliar places and then return home to their friends. We have come back to our old haunts enriched by experience. And there is no lack of an audience to hear our tales. We listen to what others have to tell us—after all we were not the only ones who saw their father holding a rifle.

A few days go by: Didube, the open field and the new house in which we live seem familiar and unchanged. We awake, as before, to the hoot of the works' siren and run to the bakery for bread. And there's Father returning home on the footpath. . . .

Pavlusha as usual leads our gang: he is best at inventing new games. We play at militiamen and policemen and relive their battles, the escape from ambush and the fight for the gorge. These games take many forms, but now, too, books have appeared in our lives. We read about the sorrows of Dickens' young characters, and the misfortunes of fleeing red Indians and other adventure stories. Books keep us off the streets: it is not easy to leave a book over which one has shed tears. Does not life repeat what one reads? And those compulsive characters, the poor of London's slums, whose misfortunes Dickens depicts in his books, cannot they be found in Didube? Only they are more ragged, poorer and hungrier. Do they not get up at crack of dawn and troop down the footpath in single file to the workshops? And when I read about the little girl who stayed with her father in prison, I visualize the fortress above the river Kura, behind whose bars I see before me the faces of my uncles Misha, Alyosha, my father's face, and the faces of so many others. . . .

But the bright sun shines alike on the city of Tiflis and on the house of the poor in Didube. You cannot ignore its summons. Our gang is already out in the street, having invented a new ending to their game. I must put away my book and run out to join them, or I may be late!

Life again offers us security in the company of our young friends.

But why has Mother come to the open field, and with her the other women from the settlement? Something seems to have disturbed them. They are waiting for the works' siren, but no siren is heard. We run after Mother along the footpath toward the works. A ring of soldiers and police surround the place.

The soldiers will not allow the women and children to approach. They raise their rifles. We stand for a long time in the burning sun, holding on to our mothers' hands. Now everything has become obvious. Many workers have been arrested and will be taken to prison—among them my father, someone whispers to me. The doors are flung open and the men come out one by one. Their faces look drawn and angry. The women surround them.

"Vaso, where's Nikolai? Where's Vanno?"

Everybody knows everybody else by his Christian name, but the men who have come out of the workshop refuse to answer questions.

"Have you seen Sergei?" Mother asks, stopping each one in turn.

"No."

Nothing is known about Sergei or about the others. Many homes will be fatherless in Didube today.

. . . Only a few months have passed since the Tzar's Manifesto. Much was promised through the Tzar's tender mercy, but little enough remained for the workers. The trans-Caucasian railways were placed under military rule. The elections to the Duma were under way and the authorities were anxious to remove all troublemakers from the works. An opportunity presented itself when the workers, driven by despair through police spies and informers, killed an *agent provocateur* in one of the workshops. The men who had shot him vanished.

On the next day during the lunch break the workshop was ringed by troops. An officer of the Tiflis sharpshooter regiment demanded the names of suspects. He arrested thirty men on a warrant, among them my father. The arrested men were then hustled into the yard in the hope that someone would betray the guilty party, but the workers refused to fall for this trick. The prisoners were then taken under armed convoy to the Ortchalsky prison some five miles away. About halfway, a detachment of sharpshooters met them. The officer in charge shouted an order to the leader of the convoy, but the prisoners reacted promptly. My father, who stood in the rear ranks, was thrust forward into the middle and a tight circle of his friends formed around him.

This was just as well, because someone had given orders to the sharpshooters to kill my father and an attempt was made to strike him. This was the usual method: a prisoner, surprised by a blow in his back, would lurch forward. A hue and cry would follow: "Oh, so you think you can escape?" and he would be finished off with either a bullet or a stab from a bayonet in his back.

. . . The arrested men have been threatened with court-martial. It is dreadful to think of the consequences.[21]

Pavel and Mother go off somewhere every day; they are trying to discover the truth of the situation and find Father's whereabouts. Pavel has become very silent and thoughtful lately. He seems to be quite grown up. We lie awake at nights. The darkness is frightening. Our life has taken a complete turn again. Pavlusha and Fedya lie side by side under the same bedclothes. I can hear them whisper: "Well, we've got to do something," says Pavlusha. "We'll have to find a way of making a living. . . ."

"Making a living? But how?" Fedya asks his elder brother.

"We can begin by selling newspapers . . ."

"Newspapers . . ." Fedya repeats.

Of course Pavel is quite right. Even I could run around shouting *Akhali Tskhovreba* [*Our Life*], which is the name of the newspaper which our friends bring to us.[22]

The railway-yard workmen who had been seized and put into the Ortchalsky prison have been told that they will be court-martialed. People expect the worst. The first victims have already been named and a number of them have been sentenced to death.

Rumors multiply: they say that some men have been shot in the Ortchalsky prison, Alliluyev among them. The prisoners' wives cannot bear this suspense any longer. They demand to see the railway administrator on whose orders the men were arrested. Why have they been sentenced to death?

The administrator receives the women. He never stops smiling as he listens to what they have to say. They fight to control their tears and their indignation. Finally, they relapse into silence and await his reply.

"I see no reason for all this agitation," says the administrator. "The prisoners appear to be in good shape and in no hurry to leave the prison, otherwise they would have revealed the identity of the real murderers."

His voice hardens as he begins to threaten. If the murderers are not handed over, all the prisoners will be despatched to Siberia. He pauses and then glances around the women: "Incidentally, relatives could help the prisoners. Tell us who was responsible for the murder and your husbands will be released . . ."

The women exchange glances: they understand each other. No, they won't accept their husbands' freedom at this price. The administrator fails to discover anything and the women leave.

The days drag by painfully, filled with rumors which drift in from the streets or scraps of information brought to us by our friends. The same question repeats itself again and again over the persistent noise of Mother's sewing machine: "What will happen to Father? What will become of us?"

Pavlusha seems to have grown more mature in these days. He carries out Mother's instructions, or prevents us from making too much noise when we grow forgetful, and when Mother pauses for a moment at her sewing machine and drops her head into her hands, he comes up to her and says softly: "Don't, Mother . . ."

She glances up at her eldest son, straightens herself, and the sewing machine turns rhythmically again. But it is difficult for this one noisy machine to feed so many mouths. We hear that friends have found Mother a job as a sales assistant in a shop, the first cooperative store run by the railway workers. We lie in bed discussing this new development.

"We must try to help Mother," Pavlusha says. "Get a job packing and delivering parcels . . ."

We go off to sleep with this blissful prospect in our minds. In the morning we hear women chattering excitedly on the balconies. Mother's voice sounds loudest and most confident. Good news has arrived: the prisoners are alive and permission has been granted to visit them. Tomorrow we shall see Father. . . .

We go first by horse-tram and then on foot across a sunbaked field toward the prison. We are not alone. There are people ahead and people behind us, trying to catch up with us. They are the prisoners' relatives. The road seems endless. Little Nadya begins to tire and Pavlusha picks her up and carries her on his shoulders.

"There's the prison. Over there . . ."

The Ortchalsky prison does not resemble the familiar Metekh prison-fortress. Low, gray buildings appear behind the walls, with barred windows and a heavy bolted door. I begin to tremble: I had heard so much about this death house where the condemned await their last hour!

"Niura, look." Fedya jolts me.

I turn around. Fedya is standing in front of an upright post with a heavy crossbeam.

"It was here they were hanged," someone says. "They refused to have their eyes bandaged. They placed the ropes around their own necks and kicked away the stools from under their feet."

They refer to the men who had been condemned to death. I have heard so much about them. I do not remember their names, but I know that they died for truth and freedom, for the same cause that my father and his friends have been sent to prison. They had struggled against evil and injustice and were slain, just as Sasha [Nikiforov] was killed, and those others whose bodies were found on the woody hillside. . . .

I look at my brothers Pavel and Fedya; they cannot take their eyes off the hideous scaffold.

We stand outside the locked gates of the prison for a long time. Will we see Father? We cannot show our impatience as we stand silent under the burning sun.

Finally the prison doors open slowly and we see the yard before us. Someone whispers: "This is where they bring them out for exercise. . . ."

At the moment the yard is empty. Its entire length has been roped off by warders. Armed guards take their place by the rope and then the prisoners' relatives are allowed to approach. The prisoners enter the yard. They come near,

Sergei and Olga Alliluyev with their children in 1900

Olga Alliluyeva with the children, Pavel, Fedya, Nadya and Anna, in 1904

Nakhalovka, a working-class district of Tiflis where illegal cells held their meetings in 1898–1900

The Metekh Fortress (Tiflis prison) where Sergei Alliluyev was confined

Управленіе.

3) Во весь ростъ, стоя,

Tiflis police registration card for Sergei Alliluyev

Revolutionary circle among Tiflis railway workers led by Sergei Alliluyev, 1902

Leonid Krassin, 1900

Shelgrenov

Victor Konstantinovich
Kurnatovsky

Hippolite Franceschi

Lado Ketskhoveli

Sasha Tsulukidze

Joseph (Soso) Stalin, 1900

Radio Times Hudson Picture Library

Nadezhda Stalin

impatiently searching for familiar faces in the crowd. We cannot see Father. Where is he?

"Where's Sergei?" Mother asks.

But we have already seen him. All four of us cry out: "Father!"

He smiles to us from afar. Nadya stretches out her arms toward him, but the prison guard does not take his eyes off the prisoners. Father straightens up.

"Well, what's happened? Has sentence been passed?" Mother asks.

"It's nothing, nothing. Keep calm."

The prisoners have already been told their fate. They have been sentenced to exile somewhere in the far north.

Chapter Fourteen

Stalin's Mother

In the fourth month following his arrest Father is sentenced to exile. We get ready for the long journey northward to the province of Archangel. Every evening our family debates the situation. We listen to what Pavel has to say; he has a most amusing way of depicting the future.

"There will be snowfields—the tundra—and forests of fir and pine trees," he assures us as if he can already see those snow-covered fields. "And as for the wild life—why there'll be reindeer and polar bears! Father and I will go out hunting and bring Mother rabbits to cook for dinner. We can always sell the skins afterward. . . ."

We get carried away. Fedya's eyes shine brightly, but he is not too sure if they will take him hunting. Of course they will. Pavel will speak to Father and arrange everything: Fedya will be quite a big boy by then . . .

But Pavel never got around to making a special plea on Fedya's behalf. We never saw the tundra, nor did we try our luck as huntsmen in the forests of the north. In fact, we never went to Archangel. Instead, we fell ill with measles. For a few days we tossed feverishly in our beds, then our temperature dropped. But we stayed in bed for a long time feeling very weak and looking very thin and all day long Mother's head could be seen bending over first one bed and then another. One night, just before going to sleep, I hear Mother whisper: "Niura, don't say a word, but Father's returned. He escaped from exile. I am going out to meet him. Lie still and listen. Pavel and the little ones are asleep. Don't wake them."

I raise myself from the bed, barely able to suppress a joyful cry. Mother looks at me.

"Now keep quiet! Quiet! You understand?"

Of course I understand. Mother hurriedly puts on a shawl and slips silently out of the room. I get up; it is impossible to sleep. The room is silent except for the peaceful breathing of the sleepers. I cannot contain myself much longer.

"Pavlusha . . . Pavlusha . . ." I say in a penetrating whisper, awakening my eldest brother.

He rubs his eyes and raises his head.

"Father has come back, Pavlusha."

Pavlusha sits down on my bed. We hug each other closely and listen.

"Father has run away from exile, but what will happen to him now? How did he escape? They are probably trying to catch him. We must try to hide him."

We hear cautious footsteps outside on the gallery and forget about everything. We jump off the bed, run to the door and, taking Father by the hands, pull him into the room.

A bed is prepared for him on the balcony. At the slightest hint of danger, he can lower himself down and escape into the street through a door. The night goes by uneventfully, but the morning brings trouble. The police are searching the rooms and apartments belonging to the railway workers. The news spreads from house to house as if carried by wireless. The police are already searching our yard; the street has probably already been cut off. We can hear the stamp of boots on the gallery connecting the doors of the other apartments. Where can Father hide? Mother makes a gesture and Father slips behind the door of our second room. Mother sits down to her sewing machine and we remain in our beds.

The policemen open the door to this room.

"Ah, so it's you."

They know her only too well.

"Where's your husband?"

Mother stops turning the sewing machine at that question and lifts her head. I can see her eyes are filled with tears.

"But you know very well he's not in Tiflis. He's been exiled. Exiled! You know that, too. I am here alone with my sick children"—Mother gestures around the room—"Look for yourselves. They are ill."

There was something so convincing about Mother's explanation that the police merely glanced around the room and left. We did not make a move until their footsteps died out.

Father stayed in Tiflis for a few days. It was impossible to remain much longer. Someone had babbled about his return, and he had to leave.

Sergei Alliluyev then turned up in Baku where he was arrested at a meeting of the Bolshevik committee in that city. His wife came to Baku, and with the help of Leonid Krassin and others, arranged bail for her husband. Alliluyev went underground in Baku, living under an assumed name, while his family moved from Didube, where they were well known, and took a room in a small house belonging to a washerwoman. At the end of the street where they lived ran the funicular railway to the top of St. David's Hill, with its ancient church and cemetery. The crest of this hill was dominated by a gigantic granite statue of Stalin.[23] *In her memoirs, Anna Alliluyeva recalls a visit both she and other members of her family paid to the grave of Stalin's mother, shortly after the latter's death in 1938. Although Anna Alliluyeva does not mention the fact, Stalin's mother "Keke," as she was affectionately known in family circles, remained a pious Christian all her life. Anna Alliluyeva allows herself, however, a hint of criticism in Stalin's separation from his mother, his rare visits to Tiflis where she lived, and his refusal to allow a cross to be placed on her grave.*

Our entire family paid a visit to the cemetery on St. David's Hill. There were a number of new graves to be seen among the ancient headstones. A plaque stands on a small granite pedestal, on which is written in Georgian "Ekaterina Georgievna Djugashvili." Only recently I had visited this dear old lady in her small modest apartment on Rustaveli Prospect [the main street of Tiflis].

My meeting with her is firmly fixed in my memory. It would indeed be difficult to forget Granny Keke, who was always so kindly and serene. Her many-sided character contained those remarkable traits people develop after a long life of endurance, worry and sorrow which fail to break them.

Ill health, and the fact that she was accustomed to a warm climate, compelled Ekaterina Georgievna to live in Tiflis, away from those who were near and dear to her. She did not complain of her loneliness, but I could feel from the persistent way that she asked for detailed news of her own people that the separation weighed heavily on her and that all her thoughts were with them there in Moscow.

She would gaze intently at the photo which I had brought her as if trying to fix it in her memory.

"He's grown . . . eyes like his father's," she said, continuing to look at the photograph of her grandson who had been brought to Tiflis when he was still quite young.[24]

On the table in her modest, unpretentiously furnished room, lay numerous Georgian-language newspapers.

"As you see," she said, "I read them every day. . . ."

She then spoke about the current news of the day. One could not help but feel she scanned the newspapers daily because she wished to find news of the work and activities of those close to her.

Ekaterina Georgievna lived a long full life and had known hardship, but she was always modest and undemanding.

I remember seeing her once at Borzhomi [a watering spa] where she had come for a cure. Despite her advanced age and ill health this frail-looking woman held herself very straight as she sat on one of the park benches. Under a tightly drawn black kerchief which covered the hard velvet ring of her headdress [Georgian national costume] her dark gray eyes sparkled, revealing an active mind. I expressed my surprise that she should be dressed in this fashion on an unbearably sultry day.

"I'm afraid I've no choice," Ekaterina Georgievna replied; "everyone knows me here. . . ."

Chapter Fifteen

Champagne, Heaven and America

After a period of prison and in exile in Archangel from October 1906 to April 1907, Sergei Alliluyev settled in St. Petersburg where he was joined by his family. Olga Alliluyeva, his wife, and the four children welcomed this move although, as Anna Alliluyeva puts it, "instead of changing towns, we began changing apartments." The problem of educating the children now became pressing, but disaster again struck the family.

The first winter we settled in Petersburg was not a happy one. Mother fell seriously and dangerously ill and was taken to a hospital. Without her constant care and attention our apartment became like an orphanage for many a day. Pavlusha and I did what we could to replace Mother in taking care of the younger children. We set feverishly to doing the chores which we recalled Mother had done. Pavlusha was now in his fourteenth year, but he did not scorn to do any "girlish" job. Good, considerate and loyal Pavel!

Once we were discovered washing the floors by one of our neighbors. This young girl asked: "Why are you washing the floors yourselves?" It was obvious that she considered such work below one's dignity. "Surely you have a maid?"

"No, we haven't," Pavel replied. "We wash the floors ourselves, and there's nothing to be ashamed in that. If they have to be washed, we wash them." He plunged the washrag into the bucket of water with renewed vigor.

When Mother returned from the hospital, a cholera epidemic broke out in Petersburg. The "cholera cart" took someone away each day from the poverty-stricken cellars below our apartment house. One day I, too, was put into this cart. I had eaten some apricot kernels which caused food poisoning, but the doctor, frightened of the epidemic, sent me off to the barracks hospital as "a suspected case." I lay among the sick, crying my heart out from fear and loneliness, listening to their shrieks and groans.

Finally, after my recovery, we were sent to school. We were again living in a new apartment, this time on the Fourteenth Line of the Vassilievsky Island. Mother had selected a primary state school for Pavel, Fedya and myself. Religious instruction was the main subject at this school. Each day we were taught about God and the miracles which He performed. We were constantly admonished that this God wished us to love the government and the Tzar. In the prayers which we offered up to God, we prayed for the Tzar. But we held a contrary opinion of the Tzar for a long time. It was not for nothing that the First Revolution had colored our childhood.

"The workers' blood—that's what he demands, that's what the Tzar requires," Pavlusha used to say.

We dreamed of growing up quickly to take part in the people's struggle waged by our older friends. But we had also learned to keep quiet about many things. Fedya and I obediently learned by heart the parables and texts taken from the Bible: after all the Gospel was fascinating, taken as a fairy tale.

But Pavlusha reacted quite differently. His rebellious spirit had to find some outlet and the dreary, formal methods of instruction fanned his stubborn, boyish opposition. He detested the spirit of resignation which they tried to inculcate at school. Pavel mocked the priest and his parables and laughed at the instructors who so movingly extolled the Tzar. During lessons he read adventure stories; these were closer to his temperament than the dreary and unrewarding lessons he had to learn by rote. Pavlusha had to be removed from school. He continued to study at home, taught by student friends, preparing for his final examinations.

Fedya and I completed our primary schooling and prepared to enter a gymnasium [a secondary school], which was Mother's fondest wish. She loved to repeat jokingly: "A fortune teller once told me that you would become savants."

But not everyone agreed with Mother. Shortly before entering high school, I went to ask for some kind of reference from our old headmistress. She looked me over and said with an unpleasant sneer: "Well, fancy that! So you're going to high school? Since when have children of the poorer classes begun to aspire to that?"

I was sent to a private gymnasium, which was considered to be "progressive." It was not so routine-ridden as my previous school, but we had the same religious instruction, the same prayers. The school chaplain tried to instill in the girls' heads that everything in the world was secure and happy. He told us about the bliss which awaited the good in heaven.

"But why doesn't God allow sinners into paradise even for a little while?" I once asked in class. "After all, God is all-merciful."

My classmates turned around to look at me: how had I summoned enough courage to ask such a question? The priest was usually kindly disposed toward me because he rather liked my religious-sounding name.[25] He was in no way put out: he could speak for God since he knew Him very well.

"There's a perfectly simple explanation, children. God does not allow sinners into Heaven for their own good. So that you can grasp this point, try to imagine Heaven: it is as bright as at your school ball, music is playing, the place is filled with gorgeous decorations. You whirl on the dance floor in your ball gowns. Suddenly a beggar girl appears at the ball; she is dirty and ragged. She would feel so uncomfortable in her rags among all you clean, sweet-smelling young ladies. And you, too, would be embarrassed by her presence. Surely it is obvious that she is out of place and that she would be much happier among those as poor, as unfortunate and unwashed as herself. A sinner in Heaven would feel as much out of place as this beggar girl."

The priest came to the end of his discourse, convinced that we had been persuaded by his little allegory. He was a kindly, well-intentioned man and probably believed sincerely in what he had said. He promised us paradise in heaven! And what about life on earth? Here too, the poor and the ragged were excluded from paradise. How were they to blame, those for whom life on earth was a hell? There were many questions I should have liked to have put to the priest. But one had to be circumspect, otherwise one could be asked: "Where did you hear about this? Do they talk about this at home?"

I thought to myself with pride: let him make promises about paradise in heaven, while Father, Mother and all our friends fight to create paradise on earth . . . for everyone without exception.

I knew very well that the struggle was unceasing. Our apartment had long become a general meeting place. Friends from the Caucasus came to visit us, as others did who worked with Father or were connected with Bolshevik and working-class organizations in Petersburg. The most stringent precautions had to be observed during those years—the entire police apparatus, fearful of revolution, placed every suspect under surveillance. It was risky to hold meetings and gatherings in our apartment: it was too well known to the police who soon had it under their eye. They were particularly anxious to catch up with one of our comrades who lodged with us. He slept in the front room with Pavlusha.

One night we were awakened by loud knocking at the door. We knew immediately that it was the police, who were not inclined to ring the doorbell in these days. They had recently suffered something of a calamity. When a policeman had rung the bell at a door of one suspect an infernal machine had blown up, killing two of the gendarmes. Now the gendarmes were of two minds about pressing doorbells.

Father opened the door and the policemen entered. But the man they were searching for had been warned and had left early that morning. The police went through the flat with a fine-tooth comb, looking under beds and into all the cupboards. But we had managed to burn all illegal literature and documents and Mother succeeded in hiding the other stuff somehow.

Once more we were compelled to move apartments. From the Fourteenth Line we moved to the Fifteenth Line of the Vassilievsky Island. And misfortune suddenly struck us again: Father became seriously ill. He was taken to a hospital, and on the third day Mother was summoned to be told that Father's condition was hopeless. But the doctors added: "The patient's life could be saved, but he requires special attention. He needs a nurse . . . and it would be good if you could get him some champagne to fortify him. But one doubts whether your financial situation could meet these requirements."

Of course we had not the means to buy champagne. But we were not alone: we had the organization and friends who came to our assistance. Our friends Flerov, Jibladze, Golubev, Galkin and Afanasev took turns looking after Father on his sickbed. Champagne, medicine, and the best possible attention—everything was found and paid for. Father began to improve slowly.

The spring came, and with it examinations at the gymnasium. Fedya and I pored over our books from morning to night. It was more difficult for Pavel. He was preparing for examinations for a course in a comprehensive school [where the humanities and sciences were taught: a so-called real gymnasium]. In one year he covered the studies of a number of classes. He was silent and concentrated and closeted himself away from us. There was no need to ask him any questions: we knew what he was experiencing. On the eve of his first examination, he left the house and did not return. We concluded that he might have gone to spend the night at a friend's house. But when he did not turn up the next day, we became desperately alarmed. We began recalling Pavel's strange behavior. I remembered that shortly before he left, I had noticed that he spent some time tying up a bundle. Curiosity had got the better of me.

"Where are you off to, Pavlusha?"

"To the public baths," he had replied briefly.

We had all noticed how confused and scatter-brained Pavel had seemed in the last few days. Mother began making inquiries among his friends. But no one knew anything about his whereabouts. Only after relentless cross-examination did one intimate friend of Pavlusha's admit that he knew where he had gone, but he had given his solemn promise to remain silent. Finally he told us everything. Pavel had decided to begin the kind of life he had read about in his books, filled with travel, struggle, danger and adventure. This is what he craved for: sea, ships, new places . . .

"Don't bother to look for him. He has run away to America," his friend concluded.

"But from which railway station did he leave?" was all that Mother asked him.

Our friends Matveyev and Vilinson went after

Pavlusha. They grabbed the runaway at the Tosno station. Pavel returned. He began work in earnest, wanting to get closer to revolutionary circles. Father understood Pavel's feelings.

"Let him take a good look at the life of working people and take a dip in that ocean of misery," Father used to say.

Chapter Sixteen

The "Fiery Colchian" Returns

Pavel went to work as an assistant mechanic in the cable network of the electricity station where his father was made a head of section in 1911. As an experienced technician in this field, Sergei Alliluyev's material conditions improved. In a tall house on Sampsonievsky Prospect in St. Petersburg his family now enjoyed the privacy of two rooms; another two rooms were set aside for a mechanical repair shop. Anna and her sister Nadya busied themselves collecting money from Bolshevik sympathizers, with which their mother bought food and clothes to be sent to Stalin, Y. Sverdlov and I. F. Dubrovinsky, who had been banished to the remote north of Russia or to Siberia At the end of June 1911, Stalin completed his term of exile in Solvychegodsk in the province of Archangel, and turned up in Petersburg early in September. Lenin's "fiery Colchian"[26] *still had no official standing in the inner circles of the Bolshevik party: he was co-opted [not elected] to the Central Committee on Lenin's recommendation in February 1912, by which time he was again arrested. Anna Alliluyeva writes about her impressions of Stalin, her future brother-in-law.*

One day, early in September 1911, the front-door bell rang.

"Open the door, Niura," Mother called from the next room. I ran past the repair shop where the duty mechanic was talking to someone on the telephone, and opened the front door.

"Oh, it's you—Sila! Please come in."

I loudly expressed my pleasure at seeing our grown-up friend Sila Todria, but suddenly stopped in my tracks when I saw a stranger standing behind the shortish Todria. The stranger was very thin in a black overcoat and a soft felt hat. When he stepped into the corridor I looked more closely at his pale face and attentive hazel-gray eyes under the thick, sharply curved eyebrows.

"Is your father at home?" asked Sila. "My friend and I would like to see him."

"He should be back shortly. Come in. Mother is in the dining room," I said.

They both went into the dining room, and Sila introduced the stranger to her.

"Meet our comrade—Soso," he said.

I hesitated about following them into the room when I heard Sila lower his voice: he addressed Mother softly, and I felt that my presence might not be welcomed.

It was almost suppertime but Father had not yet returned. The two men waited for him in the dining room. Sila came into our room for a while, chatted, looked through our books, and made a few jokes. The man whom he called Soso remained in the other room reading the newspapers which were lying on the table. Through the half-opened door we could hear his somewhat muffled voice talking to Sila in an abrupt but unhurried tone of voice.

Father returned home late but greeted his guests with undisguised pleasure. He shook Soso's hand for a long time and said something to him and Sila. The muffled voice replied mockingly, rolling out his words: "Well, well . . . you seem to have them on the brain!"

"Take a look yourself through the window," said Father. The three of them went over to the open window which faced Saratovskaya Street.

"Well, can you see them now?" Father continued. "They can't fool me. I recognized them as soon as I approached the house."

We found ourselves listening attentively to the conversation. Then the door of our room burst open.

"Hey, there, you children," Father called us, "go down to the yard, one by one, and see if there are a couple of men prowling around—you know—the ones in bowler hats. . . ."

I was the first to run down. After taking a few steps I spotted one of the men Father mentioned standing in the arch leading to the yard. The second one I recognized in the street facing our windows. I ran all the way to the corner shop trying to look as if I had come on an errand; on my way back, I again noticed the two detectives. I described everything I had seen when I came home.

"We'll have to wait awhile," said Soso.

We now knew that this was the same Soso about whom we had heard so often from our friends. Soso—the well-known revolutionary whom Father had already met in Tiflis and Baku; Soso, who had been arrested and exiled several times but who had always managed to escape. And now he was on the run from the far north and the police were already after him.

Fedya also went down into the yard and told us on his return that the two bowler-hatted men were still patroling in front of the house.

Evening approached and it was already getting dark. Another mechanic came on duty for the next shift, and the fitter Zabelin came into the dining room. The door of our room was closed, and we dared not ask any more questions; we were just getting ready to go to bed when we heard Soso exchange goodbyes with Mother and Father.

. . . A few days later Sila dropped in again. He appeared to be gloomy and worried.

"He has been arrested," he replied to our unspoken question. Later we heard from Stalin, Sila and Father what had happened in those few days. Here is the sequence of events:

Stalin had arrived in St. Petersburg [from Volgada, a town about midway between Archangel and Petersburg]. It was a gray, drizzly morning. He left the Nikolaevsky station and decided to wander around town. He had friends in Petersburg and he hoped that he would bump into one of them in the street. It would be safer than going to their homes.

He walked the streets in the rain for the better part of the day. In the evening he again returned to the Nevsky Prospect [the main thoroughfare in St. Petersburg].

The crowd was beginning to thin, the electric advertisement signs were being switched off, and fewer and fewer cabs went by as he climbed from the Liteyny to Fontanka for the third or fourth time. Only then did his attention fall on one passerby. He followed him, greeting him in a low voice. He was speaking to Sila Todria, who was returning home after his shift at the printing works. Sila was about to explain out loud when Soso stopped him: "Let's go. Let's go," he said to Sila, and they began walking together.

"It's extremely dangerous," Sila told Stalin. "After Stolypin's[27] assassination the entire police force has been alerted. All front doors and gates have to be closed by midnight. I'll have to wake the concierge and we'll have to produce our identity cards. Apartment keepers are frightened of anything suspicious. . . ."

"Let's find furnished rooms, somewhere not too far from here," Stalin suggested.

He took a furnished room on Goncharnaya Street. The

porter eyes him suspiciously and carefully inspected his identity card on which he was described as "Piotr Alexeivich Chizhikov."

In the morning Sila came to meet him as arranged. They went out together and walked in the direction of Sampsonievskaya [where the Alliluyevs lived]. They did not notice that they were being followed. Two plain-clothes policemen, whom Father later saw in front of our house, walked behind them.

That evening Stalin managed to elude the detectives. The fitter Zabelin, who left the apartment with him, took him through the back streets to his place on Lesnaya Street. Stalin stayed the night there, made the necessary contacts with people during the following day and evening, and returned to his furnished rooms on Goncharnaya Street so as not to embarrass his friends. At dawn he was awakened by a loud knock on the door.

"Why don't you let me sleep?" he shouted. But there was a summons from the corridor for him to open the door. It was the police, and he was arrested.

Now that we knew Soso and had seen him and spoken to him, we were even more interested to hear our friends talk about him. They always spoke of him in such a way as to make us understand that Soso was one of the most important and most courageous of revolutionaries. Sila told us that in Batum, where Soso led the workers in a street demonstration, they gave him the nickname of "Koba," which in Turkish means "Fearless." That word "Koba" remained as his nickname.

"The police could never manage to keep Koba in his place of banishment," Sila Todria used to say.

Koba ran away in 1903, and in the summer of 1909 he again escaped from Solvychegodsk.

On that occasion, too, he turned up in Petersburg. Father said that Soso wrote to him before his escape, asking for our address. Father answered immediately giving full details, telling him where to find us. We were then living on the corner of Glazovaya and Borovaya streets.

Having sent off that letter Father expected Koba to arrive at any moment, but a month passed, then another, and still there was no sign of him.

It was already summer. We were in the country with Mother when one day Father happened to walk down Liteyny Street. It was a typical gray summer day in St. Petersburg, filled with busy people pushing their way through the crowds amidst the rumble of the tramcars. Father walked in the crowd without looking at anyone. Suddenly someone crossed his path. Father looked up, irritated at the passerby, and then was struck speechless for a moment. Nonchalantly, with a barely perceptible ironic smile, Soso stood right in front of him.

As they walked side by side, Soso said: "I came around to your apartment a couple of times, but didn't find anyone at home. I thought I might bump into you in the street—and there you were, as large as life, walking toward me . . ."

Where would he go now? "Soso looked so pale and exhausted," Father recounted. "I simply had to find a place where he could get some rest."

He suddenly had an idea. He would take him to the "Hole" [a basement in the house of the shipowner Kolobov, where Konon Savchenko, a Bolshevik, worked as a porter]. The "Hole" happened to be quite near. It took them only a few minutes to reach Kolobov's house. Konon was at home and there was no need to give him any explanations. Uncle Konon looked at Father, at the guest he had brought with him, and immediately began laying the table. Then they put Stalin to bed behind a chintz curtain and began considering what they should do next.

"It would be best to take the comrade to Kuzma, at the horse guards' barracks," said Konon; "otherwise if the police happen to look in, they might not believe that he is a fellow countryman of mine from Smolensk."

That evening they took Stalin to the horse guards' barracks where Kuzma Demianovich had two self-contained rooms in the outbuilding reserved for volunteer guardsmen. His family was away in the country, and only a young lad, a relative, remained in his rooms.

Here in the outbuilding next to the barracks beside the Tauride Park where cabs frequently dropped off court officials, Stalin spent about two weeks.

He often went into the city to visit his friends and would stroll serenely by the guard at the barrack gates, holding the regimental roll-call book under his arm.

Father also told us about a meeting he had with Koba in Baku in 1907 [July]. Koba had just returned from the London Congress. Father had been arrested shortly before together with members of the Baku committee of the party, but as there was no evidence against him, he had been released on bail. This was Father's seventh arrest and his friends advised him to hide from the police.

Father talked over his problems with Stalin in a clay Tartar house with a low ceiling, on the Bailov Peninsula, which Stalin had rented from a Turkish houseowner. He asked Stalin what to do. He told him that he had been invited to Petersburg by Krassin, using the identity card belonging to a comrade, Rudenko. Stalin asked Father how he would make his way to St. Petersburg and what he intended doing there.

"Well," he said as they parted, "it seems you ought to leave. I wish you a safe journey." Then he added, "By the way, take this money; you'll need it."

Father tried to refuse, explaining that he was amply provided with funds, but Soso repeated firmly and calmly: "Take the money; you have a large family, children. You must look after them."[28]

. . . I remember the frosts, the snowdrifts, the icy sledge paths of that winter. In February [1912], at Shrovetide, the streets were filled with low Finnish sleighs decorated with ribbons and jingling bells.

"Jump in and I'll give you a ride!" Finnish sleigh drivers cried out, waving their whips.

The stumpy little horses raced along the icy roads made hard by traffic, shaking their plaited manes, carrying their load of laughing passengers.

"Who'd like a sleigh ride? Well, get dressed and hurry—we're leaving right away!"

We all jumped up, shouting with excitement. We had just been sitting glued to the window, admiring the sleighs as they raced by, and suddenly we were invited to take a ride ourselves! And we were invited by none other than Koba—Soso himself! During this visit to Petersburg [Stalin's fourth escape from exile] he often comes to see us. We now know Soso more intimately. We know that he can be simple and gay and that, although he is usually uncommunicative and reserved, he can also laugh and joke boyishly and tell amusing stories. He sees the funny side of people and imitates them to such perfection that everyone roars with laughter.

"Come on, all of you, get dressed! We're all going!"

Fedya, Nadya, Fenya, our maid and I grab our fur coats and run downstairs. Soso calls out to a sleigh driver: "What about giving us a ride?"

We take our places in the sleigh. Every word that is uttered makes us laugh. Soso laughs with us at everything: at the way our driver praises his emaciated little horse, at our screams as we bump over a snowdrift, certain that at any moment we will take a tumble.

The sledge glides down Sampsonievskaya Prospect, past the station from where a small steam train takes passengers to Lesnoy.

"Stop! I'll get off here—and you can ride back home." Jumping off the sleigh, Stalin walks hurriedly to the station.

. . . He came to visit us that winter together with Yakov

Mikhailovich Sverdlov. They had run away together from the Narym Territory [western Siberia] at the end of autumn 1912. At this time at home and in the repair shop there was much talk about the forthcoming elections to the state Duma for which all political parties were getting ready. When friends gathered at our place, they mentioned the names of the candidates, discussing which of them would be backed by "our" side, and which by "theirs." Like the people around us, we read newspaper accounts of the campaign avidly and anxiously, arguing about its outcome. Most of the information we picked up from hints, and we could conclude that the Bolsheviks were using the elections to the Duma as a means of stirring up the workers in Petersburg and that secret meetings were being held in plants and factories.

I recall that Stalin dropped in on us two or three times in the morning when work had just begun in the electrical repair shop. He would sit on the sofa in the dining room, looking very tired.

"If you feel like taking a rest, Soso, go and lie down on the bed in the storeroom," Mother would tell him. "It's no good trying to snatch a nap in this bedlam . . ."

Peace returned to our apartment only late in the evening; otherwise people were constantly trooping in: mechanics on the job or friends who would sit down to tea, argue and read aloud from the newspapers.

The small room behind the kitchen at the far end of the corridor was the quietest and most peaceful place in the whole apartment. There was a narrow iron bedstead on which Stalin used to rest on a number of occasions. He would come in after a sleepless night, since illegal meetings during the campaign for the Duma stretched well into the early hours. Moreover, as "illegal" persons, both of them on the run, both he and Sverdlov would flit from one place to another, crossing street after street to confuse the Okhrana [Tzarist secret police], making their way through back alleys. If they happened to pass a workman's café they would drop in and sit over a cup of tea until two o'clock in the morning. Should they come across a policeman on his beat, they pretended to be slightly tipsy and would dive into a tearoom where they could sit it out until morning in the company of cab drivers amidst the stench of cheap tobacco and afterward make their way to some friend's apartment.

The police pursued Stalin relentlessly. Every evening he had to think of some new place where he could spend the night. On one occasion when he was leaving our apartment, he said to Mother: "Please come out with me."

Mother did not ask any questions. She put on her coat and went out with Stalin. Having plotted their course of action, they hired a cab and drove off. Stalin made a sign and Mother got out. He was evidently shaking the police off his tracks. He continued his journey alone.

One evening, he rang the door bell, and without taking off his coat, said to Mother: "Please, Olga, go to the Marinsky Theater straight away; you should be in time for the opening performance. . . ." He handed her a ticket. "I did so want to visit the theater even on one occasion, but as you see I can't. I simply dare not. . . ."

Friends were waiting for him in a theater box and he wanted Mother to pass a short message to them.

Stalin used to describe his life with Sverdlov in exile. The day the mail arrived was like a long-awaited holiday, but they had to walk several kilometers to fetch their mail. They agreed between themselves that the person who went to fetch these letters should be relieved from all domestic chores for the rest of the day.

"I liked slipping out for the mail an extra time or two," Stalin said, chuckling.

So, willy-nilly, Sverdlov had to do the housework, lighting the stove and cleaning up and suchlike.

Much later, shortly before Sverdlov's death [he died in 1919] both he and Stalin recalled those distant days.

"There were numerous occasions when I tried to fool you so as to escape from domestic chores. I'd wake up on my duty day and pretend that I was still fast asleep," said Stalin.

"Do you think I didn't know anything about it?" Sverdlov answered good-naturedly, bursting out laughing. "I was quite well aware of it."[29]

Everyone was drawn to Sverdlov because of his remarkable gentleness. He was always kind and affectionate. I can remember his dark, luxurious hair, his black beard, and the large, pensive eyes set in a thin face.

After his escape from Narym, Stalin journeyed to Cracow [then part of Austrian Poland] to meet Lenin. Much later, I heard from Stalin how he managed to make this journey without a passport. He told me laughingly how he scared two passengers who were traveling with him to the frontier. They had spent the entire journey reading aloud from a Black Hundreds' leaflet.

"I got so bored listening to them that I couldn't stand it any longer," Stalin recalled. "So I turned to them and said: 'Why do you read such rubbish? You should read other newspapers.' I don't know who they took me for, but for some reason they exchanged frightened glances, got up and without looking back left the compartment."

Stalin knew no one at the small frontier town where he disembarked. He had had to destroy the address which was given to him of the person who was to take him over the frontier. It was morning. After leaving the railway station he made his way to the marketplace. Something might turn up, some fortuitous meeting might help him, he thought. Stalin crossed and recrossed the noisy marketplace a few times. Then suddenly someone stopped him.

"You're a stranger in these parts? Are you looking for someone? Or perhaps you haven't anywhere to stay?" asked a local inhabitant, whose general appearance showed his poverty.

There was something about the man which gave Stalin

confidence. He replied: "Yes, I shall only want to stay here for a short while."

"Come to my place," said the man.

They chatted as they walked. The man was a Pole, a cobbler by profession, who lived nearby. They went into his small house; the man told Stalin to make himself at home, take a rest, and offered to share his meal with him. He was friendly but not inquisitive in any way, this poor cobbler. But he did ask if his guest had come far.

"Yes, quite a way," Stalin answered. Glancing at the tools of the cobbler's trade, lying on the low table and stool which stood in the corner of the room, he added; "My father was also a cobbler, back home in Georgia."[30]

"So you're from Georgia?" the Pole repeated. "You must be a Georgian, then. I'm told your country is very beautiful, with mountains and vineyards. And Tzarist policemen, just as in Poland. . . ." It was not clear whether the man was asking a question or merely stating a fact.

"Yes, just as in Poland," Stalin answered; "no schools in our own language, but plenty of policemen."

They looked at each other silently. Can I confide in him, Stalin thought to himself. Then, having made up his mind, he said: "I must cross the border today."

The man did not ask any further questions.

"Very well," he said. "I'll take you across myself. I know the way."

They left the hut as darkness fell. At the frontier, Stalin took some money out of his pocket. He wanted to repay him for his hospitality and assistance, but his guide pushed his hand aside.

"No," he said, firmly. "There's no need. I didn't do it for money. We are both sons of oppressed nations and should help each other." They exchanged handshakes warmly.

"Best of luck on your journey . . ."

I heard this story many years later in Moscow, after the October Revolution. When he finished telling it Stalin paused, as if trying to look back into the past.

"I should very much like to know," he said slowly, "where that man is now and what happened to him. What a pity I forgot his name and cannot trace him."

Stalin was unexpectedly arrested in February [23] 1913, when the *agent provocateur* Malinovsky betrayed him. It occurred at a charity concert organized by the Bolsheviks in the Kalashnikov Exchange. A great deal had been said about that festive occasion. Sergei Kavtaradze, who helped me with mathematics, discussed it, as did Stalin, who remarked that the evening should prove interesting. As Stalin sat at his friends' table during the concert, the police approached and took him away with them.

He was banished to the Arctic Circle, to the Turukhansk Province [northern Siberia]. We now had a new address to which to send parcels (bought through the assistance fund) and letters. Stalin recalled how happy he was when in his lonely exile he unexpectedly found a note bearing greetings from us in the pocket of his jacket. We had placed this note in the jacket when we sent him a winter suit.

He often corresponded with Father. From his letters, which we all read, we received an impression of that distant place with its cruel winters. He lived in the hut of an Ostyak fisherman in a tiny hamlet lost in the gloomy, endless tundra.

But there was not a single word about his hardships in the letters which Stalin wrote. He asked us not to send him anything and not to spend any money on him.

"Don't forget you have a large family," he reminded Father in his letters. "I have everything I need," was his usual refrain.

Here is a letter he once wrote to Mother:

25/X1 For Olga Eugenievna:

I am more than grateful to you, dear Olga Eugenievna, for your kind and good sentiments toward me. I shall never forget the concern which you have shown me. I await the time when my period of banishment is over and I can come to Petersburg, to thank you and Sergei personally, for everything. I still have two years to complete it all.

I received the parcel. Thank you. I ask only one thing: do not spend money on me: you need money yourselves. I should be happy if you would send me, from time to time, postcards with views of nature and so forth. In this forsaken spot nature is reduced to stark ugliness—in summer, the river, and in winter, the snow, and that is all there is of nature here—and I am driven by a stupid longing for the sight of some landscape even if it is only on paper.

My greetings to the boys and girls. Wish them all the very best from me.

I live much as before. I feel quite fine. My health is good as I have grown used to the conditions here. But nature is pretty fierce: three weeks ago we had up to 45 degrees of frost.

Until the next letter.

Respectfully yours,
Joseph.[31]

From Kureika [on the lower reaches of the Yenissey River where Stalin was sent in March 1914] Stalin sent a manuscript of his work on the nationalities question to Father. He asked him to send it abroad to Lenin, who was expecting the manuscript.[32]

My sister Nadya and I took the manuscript to Comrade Badayev, who sent it to Vladimir Ilyich [Lenin].

Chapter Seventeen

Pravda: a Little Truth

Every evening in our apartment on Sampsonievskaya is now devoted to study. Nadya bends over her exercise book, meticulously filling in long columns of figures. I settle down to algebra, hoping to solve some difficult problem quickly and at the same time I move aside to make room for Mother. She opens a thick volume entitled *Biology*.

"I've a whole chapter to get through," she says anxiously, settling down to work.

For some months past she has been taking a midwifery course. She was of the firm opinion that domestic work has somehow diminished this winter.

"After all, the children are quite grown up . . ."

There was some truth in this, and Mother could have taken a brief rest. But she did not like taking things easy, and with the determination which characterized everything she did, she began to study.

"I must get to know a few things, find myself a profession. It's always been my ambition," she would add a little shyly.

That is the sort of person our mother was.

She sits down at the table beside us and repeats her

lessons aloud. Fedya is our general assistant, "our prompter," Mother calls him.

Fedya has made remarkable progress at school where he received only the highest marks. As a top pupil he does not have to pay any fees at high school. He gets through his lessons at lightning speed: he only has to glance at a page to remember it almost word for word. His mental agility is such that he is always looking for some outlet.

"Well, what's the problem they've set you now?" he asks Nadya and me.

Nadya was two classes behind me, and I was one class ahead of Fedya. But Mother was his star pupil. He would go through all her exercises and sometimes he would read them aloud, and Mother would listen with unfeigned delight.

Once the lessons were over, Fedya would pick up the newspapers. This was his domain. Now that Mother was studying, part of the housework fell on Nadya and me, and if I had no time to glance through the papers, Fedya would naturally tell me about the most interesting topics.

As a result Fedya was always the first to glean the daily information from "our" newspaper. Our newspaper was the *Star* and, later, *Pravda.* Every Sunday Fedya would rush out into the street when it was almost dawn so as to grab a copy of *Pravda* from the news vendors before the issue was confiscated. And this happened quite often. Fedya would run home triumphantly, with the newspaper hidden under his jacket. He was in a great hurry to tell us that the newspaper boy barely had time to hand him a copy.

"A couple of policemen had already arrived on the spot!"

But the distribution of *Pravda* was usually handled through the repair shop in our flat. The mechanics in this workshop, Savinov and Vassily Andreivich Shelgunov, were the official editors of *Pravda.*

I recall the first conversations regarding the issue of this newspaper.

"It is a daily working-man's newspaper, with mass appeal. We should have had such a paper long before now. The *Star* after all never came out more than twice weekly."

Fund-raising plans were organized in support of *Pravda,* and each day money arrived in kopecks from its working-class supporters. Money was also raised in the repair shop. Then the first issue of *Pravda* appeared. Father himself brought home a copy, telling us that Koba [Stalin] had planned the first issue. After his escape from banishment, Stalin was staying with Polytaev, a member of the Duma who enjoyed "immunity." Stalin was tracked down and arrested on the day that *Pravda* was first issued.[33]

. . . Correspondence flowed in from all distant corners of the country, from the Urals, the far east and the Caucasus. Workers wrote about conditions of life simply and briefly. In Kharkhov youngsters worked an eleven-hour shift in a damp, rotting shed. In Petersburg a woman worker fainted in some workroom or another. She was left lying on the earthen floor because no one dared bend down to help her. Only the boss when he came into the workroom deigned to push her with his foot: "Get her out of here. This isn't a hospital."

The calm which prevailed in our girls' gymnasium seemed strangely out of place; the long line of decorous girls at prayers, the priest's sermons, all these seemed very peculiar after the news we had received from the forced-labor colony in Nerchinsk [southeastern Siberia]. Political prisoners had been manacled hand and foot for refusing to stand to attention in front of the provincial governor. Sick, consumptive, dying men were put in irons and thrown into cells with ordinary criminals.

Every day *Pravda* reported strikes. . . . There was nothing dry or impersonal about these. There was a story about a strike in a western province. Factory workers had gone on strike demanding the dismissal of a foreman who had struck a woman worker. I immediately saw in my mind's eye the house of one of those strikers in the unknown little town mentioned by the newspaper. I knew exactly what it looked like: dinner would come and the mother would put a few slices of bread on the table. One of the children would probably ask: "Is that all there is?"

More likely he would not ask that question: we never did. In the evening someone would turn up and hand something over to the Mother—and this woman would reply, just as our mother had replied: "No, thank you. There are others in greater need."

"Please take it," the friend would reply; "you have four children to consider."

Collections were constantly being taken up in aid of the strikers. Donations flowed from Petersburg factories and from our repair shop. That is how we began to understand the meaning of "workers' solidarity." This is how we felt when workers in the Lena gold mines were shot down by that faraway Siberian river, somewhere in the *taiga*[34] [marshy forests in Siberia].

We talked about the event a great deal at home. One day Pavel brought home the *Star* (this was before *Pravda* was published) and he gave it to Fedya and me to read.

We read the article which began with these words: "The country lay chained at the feet of its oppressors."

"Those are Soso's [Stalin's] words. . . . Read on further."

". . . The river of the people's movement has broken free."

"Has broken free!"

This phrase was often repeated at home.[35] Our friends, who dropped in more frequently than usual, would add: "The strikes are continuing. . . . Today another factory has joined the strike." They would mention another name.

The massacre at the Lena goldfields and the Bayliss affair[36] which filled the newspapers for several months, appeared to be two unconnected events, yet for me, at this time, they combined to give a single impression of bloody terror. On one hand were the corpses in the far-off *taiga,* and on the other the body of the brutally murdered boy, whose body was found in a dump at Kiev, and the accompanying slander which made no sense to anyone: "This child was killed by the Jews because they needed Christian blood."

The fact that some people I met outside our domestic circle accepted this slander was the most terrifying thing of all. I was amazed at the indifference which was shown by my fellow pupils in the gymnasium.

There were times when I felt like speaking out more boldly at school, to say out loud that it was all lies, that I did not belong to the world of the "haves." But the impulse would pass. We knew only too well that as children of a member of the revolutionary underground, we had to be cautious and keep quiet for the time being.

Our schoolteachers were quick to grasp what was going on in the minds of their charges. At Fedya's school, for example, which was considered "progressive," they discussed the nature of "sedition." The history teacher said: "The people who undermine peace and order are good-for-nothing young folk, loafers and layabouts, who can't find a place in society."

Fedya, who was thirteen at the time, reacted to such sentiments with hatred and fury. He waited for Pavel to return home from work to tell him about the lies he had heard at school.

Pavel was now a "complete adult" in our estimation because of his interests and activities. He continued to work at the cable network and in the evenings studied at a technical institute. Of course he was a member of a revolutionary cell. We guessed that much. Although he never said a word, there was an aura of conspiracy around him. When his friends visited our apartment, we heard them speak about such things as "the report," or "preparation for a meeting of the cell," or "picking up illegal literature."

But there were people who shared our views at school.

Once when Fedya returned from his school, I had only to look at him to guess that something had happened. A memorial service had been held in his school for one of the Romanovs. It was all very solemn. The pupils stood in ranks, dressed in black. At a given sign from the officiating deacon the pupils and teachers fell on their knees.

Then something incredible happened. One lonely figure stood up erect in the kneeling rank of senior pupils. Each time they knelt down, the young boyish figure dressed in black continued to stand upright.

"You understand," said Fedya, "he was actually expressing his protest against the Tzar and the clergy. He dared to do this, although he knew what would be in store for him. When the service ended, I ran to where he had been standing, but he was no longer there. He had been expelled on the spot from the school. . . ."

Fedya's voice was full of admiration. . . .

Pavlusha had long been treated as an equal among our friends in the repair shop. Although he was only eighteen he enjoyed indisputable authority among the elder, more sedate workers. He had a capacity of communicating with them and compelling them to think for themselves. His labors were finally rewarded when, in the summer of 1913, many factories went on strike. The Electro-Company 1886 also made preparations to strike.

The strike committee endeavored to get all workers in the various departments to come out simultaneously. Pavel was deputed to persuade the cable workers to join the strike. This was no easy task, since the cable men kept very much to themselves. The company management thought highly of them: they were better paid and many of them held good secure jobs.

Pavel talked to each man separately, trying to awaken a feeling of working-class solidarity in each one of them and to explain that demonstrations of this kind were very important.

They held a meeting in a small tearoom near the Obvodny Canal and finally made up their minds to join the strike. They drew up a list of their demands. A sudden police raid did not disturb them in the least. They staggered across the road pretending to be drunk and went into a pub. The police watched them for a while and then left.

The problem remained, however: whom were they to select to take the strikers' demands to the management? For a while everyone appeared to be reluctant and confused. Pavel, who guessed what was going on in their minds, spoke up: "We ought to send a young, unmarried man. If he's arrested, he would be the only one to suffer, whereas a married man would leave his family behind, with no one to look after it. If I've earned your trust, comrades, I suggest you send me."

The cablemen voted for Pavel, the youngest among them, to negotiate on their behalf with the management. The day after Pavel had submitted their demands he was arrested and taken to prison.

Nadya, Fedya and I were in the country after we had taken our exams that summer of 1913. We awaited Mother's arrival from town impatiently. We had heard that there had been outbreaks of unrest in the Vyborg quarter. Mother arrived, looking very distressed and lost, and told us about Pavel's arrest. We were both sad and proud at the same time. But what would happen to Pavel—what lay in store for him? Fedya impatiently asked all the questions: How did it happen? What did Pavel say when he was taken away?

I could understand Fedya's anxiety: his face expressed his fear and his pride in his brother. Why couldn't he be in prison together with Pavel? Why weren't fourteen-year-olds entrusted to do real revolutionary work?

Mother told us that they knew nothing about Pavel's arrest until a police officer arrived with his men. Father assumed that they had come to fetch him. Only when the police began burrowing in the desk drawers did Father have a chance to read the search warrant. On it was written "Pavel Alliluyev."

"If you are looking for my son—here are his things," Father said. There was nothing incriminating among the things which Father showed the police. The police left, but just before leaving the police officer in charge tried to console Mother, saying: "It's just one of those things, madam. It's typical of the younger generation. I don't even know what my own kids are up to!"

Pavel's arrest roused the cable workers, but the main object of Pavel's task had been completed: the cablemen came out on strike.

"We'll not return to work until our delegate is released," they stated.

Pavel sat in solitary for a month before he was due to be tried. He was questioned a number of times and asked to disclose the names of the strike organizers. The investigator used various tricks by bringing Pavel face to face with other arrested persons and by threatening him, but Pavel played the young simpleton and kept his mouth shut, giving no one away.

The management of the 1886 Company finally gave way: the strike threatened to close down many factories in Petersburg. Most of the strikers' demands were met, and Pavel was released from prison.

Sundays always began with Father calling us: "Get up! Get up! Breakfast's on the table! Get dressed, hurry." He would then place our shoes which he had polished to look like glass at the foot of our beds. "Look what I've done for you—you lazybones, all of you."

Father insisted that everyone should sit down to breakfast at the same time on Sundays. It was always gay and noisy:

"Yesterday at school . . ."

"Yesterday in the repair shop . . ."

On Sunday evenings the whole family went to the Narodny Dom [People's House: a concert and opera house]. We fell in love with the theater that winter, but we were first attracted to opera. Mother and her sisters sang, and Uncle Vanya taught us to accompany ourselves on the guitar. We enjoyed Georgian melodies and got to know Russian music well. But in Petersburg the world of music opened for us in a new way. We heard opera performances by such famous artists as Chaliapin, Sobinov, Battistini and Caruso.

We did not mind waiting in line all night in front of the Narodny Dom to get a ticket for *Faust*—it was a small price to pay to hear Chaliapin sing the part of Mephistopheles. The ticket cost ten kopecks [about seven cents] and the crowd was filled with lively young people, men and women students and workers. We all made friends during the night; people boasted about the autographs of their favorite "stars" and repeated the jokes made by Chaliapin, and before long it was morning.

And then we visited the Alexandrinsky Theater where we saw Savina, Davidov and Varlamov. And finally, we were exposed to the cinema. The Russian "Golden Series" [a program of early films] was being shown with such actors as Polonsky, Mozhukhin and Vera Holodnaya. But Father was opposed to the "Golden Series."

"They have a distinctly decadent influence," he would say.

But he softened his attitude somewhat when some of his friends advised him to see Zola's *The Miners*. The cinema was absolved and became one of our Sunday entertainments, which included the ice rink where Nadya cut such a dash. As soon as she stepped on the ice she seemed to float effortlessly and fearlessly across it.

But the winter also brought moments of abiding sorrow. The atmosphere in the house grew gloomy. The first question we asked when we rushed home from school was "How's Pavel?"

After his arrest and imprisonment, Pavel returned to work and to his studies. He had either overtaxed himself, or his physical condition had weakened, but he lay in hospital for almost three months. "Glandular tuberculosis" was the doctors' verdict. He was operated on, but it was not a success.

"The patient should get as much sea and sun as he can; everything else has been tried," said the professor when Father insisted on knowing Pavel's true condition.

The professor was somewhat taken aback by Father's determination to provide Pavel with these curative measures.

"But how can you afford them?" the professor asked.

Father returned home boiling with fury.

"Why didn't they tell me before what was necessary?" he demanded. He made immediate preparations to take Pavel to the Crimea, where he had friends.

"He must come back completely restored," I kept repeating to myself, but Pavel listened to all our good wishes with the apathy of a desperately sick man. The mechanics in the repair shop tried to cheer us up: "He'll pick up. He ain't the sort to give up. . . ."

Father and Pavlusha returned from the Crimea in July. Pavel was completely transformed.

"The sun did him good," Father said. "We lay on the sand and sunned ourselves as we had been advised. See what a splendid young fellow I've brought back!"

Father, too, was revived by his stay in the Crimea; a holiday after many years of trials, worries and unending work. But he got down to work immediately as his presence was requested at the cable station. The political situation also demanded his attention. The Baku strikes had continued into their third month and strikes had broken out in Petersburg workshops and factories.

Chapter Eighteen

War, 1914

On the day war was declared, the shrill cry of the news vendors shook the capital.

"War!" they shouted in the streets. "Germany declares war on Russia! . . . War! War!"

St. Petersburg was changing: it was now called Petrograd. The Tzar's portrait was carried along the Nevsky Prospect, and recruits sang: "Nightingale, nightingale, you little bird!"

Reports from the front were published and at high school small colored flags were moved on a map to show the advance of Allied forces. During handicraft lessons we knitted scarves and mittens and sewed warm underwear for the soldiers.

Everything is quiet in the Vyborg quarter. But the war has brought out fashionable crowds onto the Nevsky. They mill around the shop windows, well dressed and contented, showing off their expensive clothes and jewelry. Officers dressed in the uniform of every regiment prance by on horses. But what about the war? Was there a war somewhere?

We discuss the war at home. Mother has recently appeared in a white cap, with a red cross on her bosom. She is a Red Cross sister now; she has passed her midwifery course at the institute and is working in the hospital which was opened ceremoniously by the "1886 Company" with prayers and a banquet.

Mother tells us about the growing numbers of the wounded, the crippled and suffering who talk about betrayal at the front. The impressive spectacle of the first few days of the war has turned into a bitter sham.

"Our men have a great capacity for endurance. They are ready to do anything," says Mother. She adds, bitterly, "But they are being pushed too far!"

. . . Pavel comes home from his regimental barracks. He was mobilized early in 1915. He works as a mechanic in a military car repair works in Petrograd. When he can wangle himself leave, he comes to Sampsonievskaya and talks irritably about his job. He speaks of the sons of well-to-do Petrograd families who bribe their way out of the front line and get soft jobs in the rear. They drive up in hansom cabs just in time for roll call in the barracks. Others have to go through humiliating drill for them. The soldiers at the barracks are furious. Pavel often has a chance to have a heart-to-heart talk with them.

"Many are dissatisfied. And there's more grumbling out in the front lines . . ."

Pavel is soon sent to the front. We come to see him off at the station. This is when I first feel the proximity of the war. They stand on the platform, a line of gray overcoats, getting ready to board the goods wagons. How many are there of them? The tail of the train disappears into the distance.

"Nightingale, nightingale, you little bird!"

The same song can be heard coming from all the wagons. The soldiers sang it in their own fashion, and it sounded harsh, plaintive and sad at the same time:

> "One, two, sorrow's no misfortune!
> Canary bird sings sadly."

The soldiers waved and shouted jokes at us. There did not appear to be any despair in their faces—yet they were going to war! None of them seemed to have thought about that. They ran past, clutching kettles to fetch boiling water. Through the noise and din of the railway station balalaikas strummed and accordions droned.

Pavel stood at the door of the goods wagon and shouted to us: "Over here!"

He seemed gay, like a man who has burst out of the confines of a prison. He appeared delighted with the present we had brought him. But we could not hide our sorrow.

"Now, now, let's have none of that," Pavel said, smiling. "I'll be writing. . . . Don't forget me."

The goods wagons with the gray-coated soldiers melted from our view. We stood looking in the direction of the disappearing train for a long time. To what unknown future were they all hurrying, and with them our Pavel? The answer came through the clatter of train wheels: "Eh . . . eh . . . sorrow's no misfortune!"

The war did not prevent us from helping our friends in exile. Only one had to be doubly careful. Every month Nadya and I went to the homes of people whose addresses we had learned by heart to collect envelopes with money. Everything was getting more expensive because of the war, and the need for more money grew urgent. We again packed parcels and sent money orders to subarctic regions. Dozens of letters arrived from the exiles asking Father to help them. They were anxious to remain in contact with those who were still free. And those who were still free were constantly under surveillance.

That autumn the Bolshevik deputies of the Duma were arrested. Mother was very upset. She told us: "Petrovsky has been arrested. I've just heard about it from Dominika [Petrovsky's wife]. It seemed that all the Bolshevik deputies have been caught."

This arrest affected Grigori Ivanovich Petrovsky's family, whose acquaintance Father had made in his early days in Yekaterinoslav [now Dnepropetrovsk] where he worked with Petrovsky at the same steelworks. They both took part in revolutionary underground work in the factory there. Mother got to know Dominika during the midwifery course.

They had much in common; both were wives of revolutionaries and both had to cope with the ups and downs of life patiently and courageously. Mother used to say about Dominika: "She's so energetic, so capable . . . with such determination she could achieve anything. And she never complains and she's so full of life."

Mother obviously did not realize it, but she had sketched her own self-portrait.

The fate awaiting the Bolshevik deputies was far from clear at the beginning. A court-martial was demanded, and they were threatened with the death sentence or permanent banishment. Dominika and the wives of the other arrested men did everything possible, together with other comrades, to arouse public opinion against the arrest of their husbands whose immunity as deputies had been guaranteed by law. They demanded a meeting with their husbands and finally won their demand. The meeting was arranged between them at the entrance of the district court where the arrested men had been brought for questioning.

Dominika later described the proud and independent behavior of the deputies.

"They were ready to face up to anything. Not one of them showed any signs of weakness."

Dominika herself was prepared to face any hardship. Her beautiful face showed no trace of the heavy burden which she was carrying. Alone, she would now have to support herself and her three children.

We took the coming trial of the deputies very much to heart and discussed it at length at home. We knew Alexi Yegorovich Badayev [one of six arrested Bolshevik deputies]. Nadya and I remembered him from the time when we passed on Stalin's manuscript to him. Father was very worried about the prospect facing the prisoners: they were all close friends, brought together in the common cause.

We were relieved to hear, finally, that the trial of the deputies would take place in an ordinary court of law, which did not hand out the death sentence. We read the reports of court proceedings aloud at home; we even knew by heart passages of the defense put up by the Bolshevik deputies. They were sentenced to permanent exile in Siberia.

Shortly afterward Dominika brought us a photograph taken of the exiles in Yeniseysk while they made their way on foot from Turukhansk.

At about this same time, Stalin wrote to Father from Turukhansk. Both he and the others, Suren Spandaryan, Vera Schweitzer and Maslennikov, asked Father to give their regards to the editorial office of the magazine *Voprosy Strakhovaniya* [*Insurance Problems*]. This magazine had just resumed publication after a long break. Our friends asked that a sum of money which they had gathered by way of a contribution should be handed over to the magazine, together with their best wishes.

Chapter Nineteen

Brief Interlude

In the compartment of the military train there is the inevitable fuss which marks the end of a journey; suitcases are taken down from the rack and passengers crowd impatiently into the corridor. Nadya and I pick up our meager little bundles containing our personal belongings. The train is taking us back home to damp, gray Petrograd from Moscow. Even now, on a late summer day in August, it is foggy, and there is a pervasive drizzle.

Eight years have gone by since we first came to Petrograd, on a day as foggy and cheerless as this one. During this period we grew fond of Peter's city; it became our second home. Our friends, the school, the underground Party circles, everything which surrounded us drew us closer to it.

Four months before, in May, we left Petrograd and began our unhappy wanderings. The previous year had been a difficult one for Father. Because of the war he had to carry a heavier load at his job and the management had become more demanding and petty. The electricity station supplied power to armament factories and this threw an extra responsibility on Father. He often traveled and worked night shifts. Also the results of an electric shock which he had received some years before had begun to show, and as his nervous exhaustion increased, the more dissatisfied he became with his job.

"I'd like to go to some other place, change the job," he kept saying.

Finally, when he reached the breaking point, he wrote to his old friend Gleb Maximilianovich Krzhizhanovsky, who had meanwhile become a well-known engineer in Moscow, asking him if there was any chance of finding a job there. Gleb Maximilianovich replied immediately, saying that he could come at any time and that a job would be waiting for him. This cheered Father up immensely.

"What do you say, girls? Will you come and live in Moscow, or would you be sorry to leave Petrograd?" he asked us.

Being young, we offered no objections. The prospect of traveling, of seeing new places, of a new life altogether, excited us. Only Mother voiced some reservations; the idea of uprooting the family rather frightened her.

"It's not all that easy or simple. There's the war . . . and the children's schooling to consider. Fedya's education costs us nothing here."

Ultimately it was decided that Father should ask for leave and go alone to Moscow. Nadya and I would join him later when our school term ended. But Father did not remain in Moscow. Gleb Maximilianovich offered him a job at Bogorodsk where the first peat-burning power station in Russia had been constructed, based on Krzhizhanovsky's ideas. Nadya and I came to live with Father in May.

The power station itself stood on the outskirts of a small settlement of neat little houses scattered in a pine forest. Executives and their families lived in smart, comfortable villas; the engineers occupied somewhat simpler cottages and workers lived in modest, unpainted little houses. The village had its own water supply and the houses were fronted with flowerbeds. We liked the place: our old friends Alexander Vassilievich Winter and Krassin lived and worked there. Yekaterina Vassilievna, Krassin's wife, had often helped Mother out in our difficult days in Moscow. We were invited to play tennis at their place with other young people whom they introduced to us. Their house was always crowded with youngsters.

Sometimes we wandered around the settlement and stopped at the dug-up peat fields. Women, known locally as *torfushki,* stacked up piles of turf for drying. They were peasant women from villages around Ryazan and Mordva, dressed in linen skirts and white blouses. They never stopped singing from dawn to dusk as they worked, and this rather surprised us.

"We find it easier to work that way," explained the expansive women of Ryazan.

Prisoners of war stood by the peat extractors and dryers. They were anxious to show their friendliness by talking in Russian, which they did in a very odd way since they were not familiar with the language.

"Hello, there, how are you?" they would call to us.

Fedya came to stay with us for a short while and asked to be given a job at the power station. He was given a job at the peat drying machines where the prisoners of war also worked. The latter appeared to be very satisfied with their life in Russia and kept saying how amazed they were at the kindness of Russian people.

Every evening we went to the power station to bring Father his supper. He was working night shifts, which because of his state of health proved too much for him. His health kept getting worse, he was losing weight and growing more and more nervous. He could not sleep during the day, and after sleepless days and nights had to hurry back to his job. We knew that he could not endure the pace much longer. He realized this also and this depressed him even further. He had always been so tireless and hardy that it was difficult for him to admit that he was breaking down from exhaustion. Once or twice he collapsed, frightening Nadya and me out of our wits.

"You really shouldn't go to work, you're much too sick," we advised him, but he refused to be dissuaded. He had his job to do, he said, and somehow managed to force himself to go out to work. But one day he could not get out of bed. We went to fetch Winter and shortly afterward a doctor arrived at our cottage.

The doctor advised Father to go to Lipetsk [a large town in central Russia] which was near and where life was not too expensive. Winter and Krzhizhanovsky helped out, and Father left, but by this time he was a desperately sick man.

"I don't know how you'll manage without me," he said before leaving.

"Don't you worry about us. We'll stay here until you return," we replied light-heartedly.

But we did not feel all that easy when we saw him off. As soon as he left, we were told to vacate the cottage. We had no idea what to do. We could not return to Petrograd since the apartment on the Sampsonievskaya no longer belonged to us. Mother worked at the hospital and lived with friends. We knew how upset she would be at this turn of events. All these thoughts were whirling in our minds when we remembered Yekaterina Vassilievna Krassina, who had been so kind to us. We overcame our shyness and went to see her, telling her what had happened.

She showed great concern. "Poor children!" she exclaimed. "Let me see . . . yes, I think I have an excellent solution. Leave everything to me and don't worry about anything."

That very same day she took us to see the manager of one of the peat-processing plants. He lived in a five-room cottage by himself since his wife had gone to Moscow with their sick child.

"Take these girls in—you're here all by yourself," said Krassina, half jokingly; "they're excellent housekeepers and will look after the place for you."

"Make yourselves at home," said this kindly, responsive man, who immediately insisted on showing us around the cottage.

We chose a small room in the attic with a balcony. It now appeared that our host had met Mother and Father in 1905. He recalled that after our father's arrest, his brother had taken in Nadya, who was four at the time.

"You probably don't remember," he told Nadya, "but you and my brother traveled to Kiev together."

We did everything we could to repay our host's kindness and made ourselves useful in the house. Nadya, who was a good cook, served him some of her best dishes and our host assured us that he had not eaten so well for a long time.

Yekaterina Vassilievna often came to see us.

"Drop the housework," she would tell us, "and come to our garden. You should play a game of tennis or croquet."

We went to play an occasional game of tennis, but Nadya mostly refused the invitation.

I knew what was irking her: no matter how hospitably we were received, our problems were far removed from the carefree world of tennis and croquet. And Nadya, who was both shy and proud, could not stand any trace of condescension, however well intentioned.

"No, let's stay at home," she would propose, and we would spend the evening on our little balcony.

Autumn was approaching and our school holidays were coming to an end. Would we be able to return to Petrograd? The war was making things even more difficult and trains were becoming less frequent. But in August we received a letter from Father and we sighed with relief. It had been posted from Petrograd. Father was working again with the cable network.

"Return as soon as possible—to our new apartment which is beyond the Nevsky Gates," he wrote. "I'm not sure how you will like the place," he added apologetically, "the rooms are small and uncomfortable."

We already knew this apartment which had belonged to a friend of Father's and which we had visited. It was about four miles from the center of the city. One had to take a small steam train to reach the place, and the power station where Father worked was almost in the country, located beyond the Nevsky Gates. But nothing could put us out since we knew we were returning to our beloved Petrograd, and the sort of apartment we had hardly mattered since we would all be together again.

We did not have to do much packing but it was not easy for us to obtain train tickets for Petrograd. Finally we got onto the train and as we came to the last lap of the journey the familiar suburbs of Petrograd came into view with their stacks of chimneys and rows of gray, identical factory buildings.

I try to share my excitement with Nadya, but the train is already slowing down at the platform. Nadya leans out of the train window and cries out: "Papa!"

Yes, it is Father. He looks very preoccupied as he strides down the platform, looking into every carriage window. Fedya is beside him. My heart aches when I see Father looking so thin and hollow-cheeked. The last few months of sickness and upheaval were particularly hard on him. He was so worried about us and was afraid that his sickness would be prolonged and that he would not be able to gather his family around him and attend to our schooling. He was also unhappy because he had been forced to abandon his revolutionary activities for a while, and I knew that Father was committed heart and soul to them.

I jump out of the carriage and run as fast as I can toward him. If only I could calm him and assure him how happy and content we were!

We hug him and Fedya. Nadya exclaims: "How splendid that we have a new apartment! We'll tidy it up and make it very cozy, Papa. Please don't worry."

Chapter Twenty

News from Stalin

The house beyond the Nevsky Gates was indeed far from cozy. Father lived here alone as Mother was still working at the hospital, and Nadya and I hurried to get down to work. We cleaned, washed and scrubbed the place down, put up the curtains and laid out the tablecloths. When Father returned in the evening we enjoyed the look of astonishment on his face.

"It looks very inviting," he admitted. "You transformed the place completely. That's splendid!"

Now everything was ready for Mother's return. She arrived in the evening looking very tired but satisfied.

"I've got you all under my wing at last," she said.

She was completely absorbed by her job of nursing the wounded, who had become like close friends to her, and was deeply grieved by their misery and sad condition.

"The situation at the front is appalling. Soldiers are constantly complaining. They want an end to the war. 'What are we dying for?' they ask all the time," said Mother, sharing her impressions with us. "I look at the soldiers and I realize that they are our people, ours!"

When the wounded men got better and left the hospital, they corresponded regularly with Mother. They addressed her as "Our dear little sister" and were always seeking her advice or assistance in some matter.

Pavlusha confirmed most of these impressions of the war, which we read between the lines of his letters. He had been out at the front for the second year running. He had been laid up in a military hospital for a long time, but now he wrote to us from the trenches again.

The autumn of 1916 began in the house beyond the Nevsky Gates. I was studying at the Psycho-Neurological Institute and found the atmosphere very congenial. The students were progressive-minded and the conversations and arguments I heard there were close to my way of thinking.

Nadya went to a new high school that autumn. She had long wanted to leave the state-supported gymnasium, which she had found very gloomy, strait-laced and oppressive ever since she had attended the junior classes. Nadya had always been very vivacious, open and spontaneous, and quite high-spirited in her early childhood. These qualities did not endear her to the gymnasium.

The headmistress of this school once asked Father to come to see her. This former governess took Father severely to task for Nadya's boisterous behavior, her resounding voice and unruly hair.

"I don't find high spirits at all objectionable in children, madam," Father said, not in the least put out, "and my daughter's voice is naturally resonant, and there is nothing I can do about it."

After this interview Nadya's teachers began to find fault with her more often. This may have been due to the fact that Father had made a point of stressing his working-class origin.

Nadya was not in the habit of complaining, but from the few sentences which she let slip, I guessed that life was very hard for her at school and that she could not stand it much longer.

After her spring exams, she sighed with relief when she traveled to Moscow with me.

"It's good to be free at last!" she kept telling me in the train.

Now that she was attending a private school which was reputed to be "liberal" minded, she went off each morning far more readily.

"At least the lady teachers aren't such museum pieces, and they allow us to laugh during breaks. And the girls don't give themselves airs. . . ."

That same year Nadya fell in love with music. She had a good ear and wanted to study the piano. We had no piano at home, but Nadya managed to get into a music school near our home and each evening she went there to practice.

Our evenings at home were no longer so crowded with people. Our friends found it difficult to visit us as the little steam train which connected the Nevsky Gates with the city ran very infrequently, and it was a five- or six-kilometer walk from the center. As a result we did not see much of Vassily Andreivich Shelgunov, and we felt his absence deeply. We missed his conversation and the news which he invariably brought with him.

Nadya and I found out where he lived and went to his house near the Narvsky Gates. He was staying with relatives at the time. He was very touched and pleased to see us.

"Thanks for looking me up. . . . I find it difficult to get around (he was almost blind). The streets are so crowded, and then there are cars and trams. I doubt if I'll ever be able to visit you," he complained. And after having inquired about the family, he gave us some idea of what was happening, particularly in the Triangle factory, where his relations worked. A strike was about to begin there.

"Other factories are being drawn into the strike; they are demanding better conditions and the right to hold meetings."

He was his usual exhilarated, optimistic self.

"Believe me, people's eyes are beginning to open, as our rulers will discover to their cost."

He also told us about the reactions of soldiers returning from the front.

"Do you think they aren't aware of what is going on, why they were called on to die and shed their blood?"

We heard similar opinions from friends in the Vyborg district. Complaints and disaffection could be heard in the factories, and the army, expressed almost openly. There were continuous strikes in the Vyborg district.

"The soldiers share the strikers' sentiments," friends told us. They described how the men of the 181st infantry regiment recently joined the strikers in the Russian Renault factory. Our conversation turned to those who had been exiled. "What a pity they are not with us. . . . They could be so useful at this time," they said.

They were referring to those who had been exiled to the subarctic regions in Siberia. Letters arrived from Soso [Stalin] in which he asked Father about the fate of his friend Suren Spandaryan, who had been sent to the same village as Stalin. It appears that Stalin and Spandaryan were separated shortly afterward and Stalin was sent to another place of exile. He had lost contact with his friend and now wanted to know what had happened to him. Shortly before Stalin's letter arrived, Father had sent money to Spandaryan, but it was returned with a note stating: "Undelivered due to the decease of the addressee." Suren Spandaryan had died of tuberculosis in Siberia, and Father conveyed this melancholy news to Stalin.

Very few managed to escape from their places of banishment during this time. The authorities watched them at every step. The appearance, therefore, of Alyosha Japaridze in the city was all the more surprising; he had run away from the Yenisey province. But Alyosha was not able to come to see Father or visit us. He spent a few days hiding from the police in Petrograd and then went to Baku.

I heard all about the particulars of his escape later from Klavdia Ivanovna Nikolayevna, who had been exiled to the Yenisey with Alyosha and who helped him to escape.

"A book peddler once found his way to my hut," Klavdia Ivanovna told me, "and gave me a copy of the Holy Bible. He said that he had met a man at a lodging house who asked the peddler to sell him his Bible. He then returned the book to the Peddler asking him to pass it on to me if he chanced to come to Kazachinsk. The peddler added that the man was evidently a prisoner guarded by two armed men. I looked through the Bible many times, turning each page, and finally in a flash of inspiration I glanced between the cover and the binding, and found a letter from Alyosha. 'I am being taken to Yeniseysk for interrogation,' he wrote. 'We shall be stopping near Kazachinsk, in the village of Kargino. Try to reach me there.' "

Klavdia Ivanovna knew the penalties for leaving her place of residence without a permit, but that did not prevent her from going to Kargino, where she met Alyosha. They decided his best method of escape from Kazachinsk would be by boat.

Japaridze was sent to the village of Kameka to serve out his three years of exile, but once he got to Kazachinsk other exiles helped him to escape. One of them provided Alyosha with a dandyish outfit, a suit, shoes and a hat. Dressed in this gentlemanly outfit, he raised no suspicions and was allowed to board the boat with all due civility.

The year 1916 was drawing to its close. Ugly rumors were circulating from the Tzar's palace and were repeated on street corners and in people's houses. They concerned such unsavory characters as Rasputin, [37] Vyrubova,[38] the Grand Dukes, the Tzarina and the Tzar, whose names were pronounced with such distaste. Their very existence seemed so incredible, but they were nevertheless a living reality. Shortly afterward we heard of the death of Rasputin in Petrograd.

But the underground organization in Petrograd went from strength to strength. People met to discuss contemporary events from which they could draw the necessary conclusions. Petrograd Bolsheviks decided to welcome the new year of 1917 by holding a special gathering. The idea had been mooted at home, but finally they decided to hold the meeting at Poletayev's house.

I remember how carefully we had to approach Poletayev's two-story detached house on New Year's Eve. Many people had been invited, but we came one by one so as not to attract the attention of the police. This was going to be a very important occasion to which many Petrograd Bolsheviks, among them factory workers and professional revolutionaries, would be invited. We also knew well in advance that Maxim Gorky would be present, and we were greatly excited at the prospect of meeting the author of *Burevestnik* [*The Stormy Petrel*], *Malva* and *Chelkash*.

I cannot recall what Gorky said on this occasion, but I remember that the words he addressed to the Bolsheviks gathered on New Year's Eve 1917 at Poletayev's sounded prophetic. I shall always remember his tall figure and his gay, alert eyes, and the joyous welcome which he received from everyone present. He had come to the meeting with Demian Bedny.[39] They did not stay to the end of the meeting, but went to join their writer friends, as Gorky explained.

When they left, we asked Vassily Andreivich Shelgunov to read us some extracts from our favorite works of Gorky's, and we held our breath as we listened to *The Stormy Petrel,* whose author's hand we had just shaken.

Chapter Twenty-One

The February Revolution

An air of instability hung over the beginning of 1917, strengthening the feeling in the capital that changes were inevitable. Things could not continue as they were for much longer. Famine was imminent. Agitation had spread to the outskirts of the city, where people had grown bolder and more outspoken, paying scant attention to the police. Women refused to leave shops empty-handed.

"Our children are starving and our men are dying at the front!" they shouted, "and for what? So that the Tzar and Tzarina can indulge in orgies with their hangers-on? It's that German woman . . . that Alice,[40] who has ruined Russia. Kill the lot of them!"

People gave vent to their feelings and stones were thrown at shop windows.

"Filthy speculators! Just you wait, we'll show you how to fleece people!"

A recently introduced tax had raised the price of commodities many times over. Speculators were making fat profits from government contracts and food was disappearing from shops and street markets. There were loud protest meetings in all the factories, and strikes continued from the beginning of the year. From January 9 onward the transformer cabins in the electricity substations received news flashes that one factory after another was closing down because of the strikes. Strikers were now to be seen marching unperturbed down the streets. Such was the mood of February 1917.

On November 25, a crowd of soldiers, women, and the poor from the outskirts, could be seen moving from the Vyborg district toward the Nevsky Prospect. Tattered bits of red cloth fluttered over their heads.

"Arise you starvelings from your slumbers!" they roared.

"What's happening?" people asked in the streets.

"Revolution!" the crowd of marchers replied. "The Revolution has come!"

Nadya, Aunt Manya and I marched with this crowd as it moved toward the center of the capital.

The night before we had gone to Uncle Vanya's apartment on Sampsonievskaya, where we had remained until morning. From the expectant silence of the Nevsky Gates we were suddenly thrown into the center of events. Here they knew exactly which factories and which regiments were ready to rise in revolt, and we ourselves knew many of the strike leaders personally.

"Tomorrow is the decisive day," they kept saying.

That tomorrow for which we had waited so impatiently began with the noise of shouts and horses' hooves in the street which came to us through the windows and woke us up.

The workers were marching down the Nevsky and were already quite near. The house on Sampsonievskaya was surrounded by Cossacks.

"Come on, hurry up, let's go downstairs," we urged each other, impatient to get out into the street to join the crowds, but we were unable to get out of the yard. A Cossack detachment had blocked the road. The horses stood motionless, reined back by their riders, as if they were waiting for something to happen. They pressed the crowd into a tight mass at the gates of the entrance. We were making our way toward them when, at that moment, a man in a leather jacket emerged from the crowd, holding a revolver. Lifting up his hands, he shouted to the Cossacks: "You'd better surrender! Give up, brothers. We are many . . . come over and join us."

We recognized the man as our old friend August Toom, who worked in the Lessner factory. But his words were drowned by the officer commanding the Cossack detachment who gave the order: "Draw sabers! Advance!"

The Cossacks stayed quite still and so did the crowd. Suddenly the Cossacks whipped their horses, turned them around and disappeared in a flash through some gates opposite, and the officer was left waving his sword in the air in helpless fury. A concierge hurried up and whispered something to him, whereupon he looked over his shoulder in fear and rode off after his detachment.

We spilled out into the street. They were singing the "Marseillaise" in a crowded lorry parked at the gates, and August Toom was on that lorry.

"Where are you off to?" we shouted. "May we join you?"

"Go to the Moscow barracks. And hurry!" they replied.

We rushed down the deserted Botkin street and joined a slow-winding procession moving down Nizhniy Novgorod street, which was swelled by groups of soldiers and workmen. There were shouts from the crowd: "Three cheers for the Volynskii regiment! Come over to us, brothers! Join us! Hurrah!" as they greeted the men of the armored car units.

"Down with the Tzar!" they shouted. "Down with the betrayers!"

On a number of occasions during the procession the crowd began to waver. We were pushed back and could hear sporadic hooting quite near.

'They're starting to fire at the demonstrators,' we heard people say, but no one turned back and we pressed on regardless of the shooting.

That day, the prison gates were forced open and political prisoners were released. Early in the evening we found a group of prisoners from the Vyborg jails crowding the yard of the apartment house on Sampsonievskaya: they huddled for shelter in doorways, dressed in prison clothes and with bared heads. And these February evenings could be very cold and frosty. We did what we could to provide them with clothes and food, and ran around the apartments collecting old clothes for the prisoners. Everyone gave generously and food was brought out to the men, who stood in the middle of the yard putting on warm clothes and chewing bread. Someone had already begun organizing them into columns.

"Go and join the uprising," they were told.

A new life begins in the capital. Although no newspapers are published, posters and leaflets are pasted onto walls, telling us that all army regiments have joined the uprising and that the Tzar has been overthrown. People stand in the street to read aloud the text of the Tzar's abdication. Ministers have been arrested and there is a new government in the Duma. Crowds of Petrograders move toward the Tauride Palace [where the Duma was sitting] all day. The first open meeting has been held at the power station and Yablonsky, Father and some others have been elected to the revolutionary committee.

Father rarely comes home but spends days and nights at the power station, where the committee has reorganized the cable network of Petrograd.

As we march with the crowd toward the Tauride Palace, a car overtakes us and we spot Father.

"Father!" Nadya and I cry out loudly. We cannot help ourselves—we have not seen him for so many days. "Come to the Vyborg quarter! That's where we are!"

Father has heard us. He puts his rifle between his legs and waves to us. There is a red armband on the sleeve of his overcoat.

"Where's Mother and Fedya?" he shouts from a distance as the car rushes by.

On our way to the Duma we walk down familiar streets which I passed so many times on my way to school. But the worn pavements and carriageways look new to us. . . . The crowds, the red flags and the singing of the "Marseillaise" create this impression of novelty. A crowd has gathered at the arsenal and men with red armbands are handing out rifles. The workers at the arsenal join our column of marchers, with "Uncle Konon" at their head. As we pass Kolobov's house, with its hospitable basement, Konon Savchenko stops to inspect it.

"Take a look at that window. Can you see? That's Purishkevich[41]—we haven't dealt with him yet! Never mind, his turn'll come. . . ."

We look up at the window to which Konon is pointing and see Purishkevich's face, distorted with fear. His face is well known to us from the newspapers. Perhaps he is still hoping to get away.

Police are trying to snipe at the crowd from rooftops, bell towers, and the cupola of St. Isaac's Cathedral. But this will not save Purishkevich! These treacherous attacks merely succeed in driving the crowd wild. They drag these "Pharaohs"* from their attics and deal with them summarily there and then.

. . . Our procession continues marching across the Liteyny Bridge. Many was the time I ran across this bridge on a snowy February day admiring its broad, empty span. Now smoke and fires rise above the boulevard; the district courthouse is burning. A dark, thick stream of people moves along the street. Shots ring out too close for comfort; Nadya and I hold each other's hands firmly and press against the wall, as others do.

"They're shooting from the garret. . . . That's where they're holding out, the sons of bitches!" someone standing next to us explains.

Now they are firing down on to a truck filled with

* Nickname for the police.

soldiers. The truck pulls up and the men jump out and run into the house. The shooting comes to an abrupt end. Something falls on the pavement from a window. One of the crowd bends down and picks up some scraps of metal: fragments of armor-plate worn by the police snipers. They are escorted out of the building. They look around numb with fear and their mustaches bristle.

"Traitors!" the crowd yells at them furiously; fists are raised, but the soldiers hold back the crowd and drive off in the lorry with the policemen.

. . . Life goes on with the speed of a film track. We can hardly keep up with it. Newspapers give brief reports which barely add up to résumés. As if one can compress the present into a few words! Friends turn up at our old apartment on Sampsonievskaya to tell us about their experiences.

"The last of the regiments of the Petrograd garrison which still hesitated, the Semenovsky and Jäger regiments, have now placed themselves at the disposal of the new government," the newspapers reported. That evening Uncle Konon told us how the Semenovsky regiment (which had played such an inglorious part in putting down the 1905 revolution) came to submit to the authority of the Duma.

Uncle Konon had worked for some years on the drill ground of the Semenovsky regiment. When the workers began to move from the outer suburbs into the center of the city, the officers of the regiment locked themselves up in their mess. They knew only too well that they should not show themselves out in the streets. Uncle Konon stood by the door of the mess room and listened to what the officers were saying. They called the workers "scum" and a "dirty mob," but the regimental commander Nazimov tried to calm them down, assuring them that the revolt would shortly be brought to an end.

"The regiment will not let us down. They'll settle with

these insurgents. We have plenty of ammunition, and I have only to give the word," he said.

Uncle Konon wanted to test the accuracy of the colonel's words.

The regimental barracks was separated from the street by some railings. A crowd of officers and men in battle dress milled around. Machine-gun barrels could be observed sticking out of the barracks' windows. There were also a few NCOs sauntering around the yard. Uncle Konon climbed onto the railings and began addressing them. The NCOs and a few soldiers came closer and a crowd of people soon gathered at the entrance to the barracks.

"What are you waiting for, brother?" he began. "Don't you know what's happening? Are you going to be the people's executioners as you were in 1905?"

They listened to him in silent approval at first, but his last words were challenged by some soldiers, who said impatiently:

"It's not true! We're also on the people's side!"

Someone else chipped in: "The trouble is we've got no one to lead us."

A group of men ran out of the barracks.

"Come off that fence and help us!"

Konon climbed down from the railings.

"Where can I find the trumpeters?"

The trumpeters were found and as soon as they sounded the regimental march, the soldiers fell into line in the street. People immediately surrounded the soldiers, and many had tears in their eyes as they embraced them.

"Thank you, brothers. You did not betray us! Stand by us! Prove that you were deceived in 1905."

A delegation from the Jäger regiment approached Uncle Konon. Their barracks were not far off and news had reached them quickly that the Semenovsky regiment had joined the insurgents. Delegates came to ask him to lead them also.

Suddenly a fire broke out on the opposite side of the street. The police station had been set alight.

"Release the prisoners!" the men of the Semenovsky regiment demanded. They were let out and the regiment marched off to join up with the Jäger battalions. These two regiments, consisting of twenty thousand men, moved toward the Duma with Uncle Konon at their head.

The city turned out to pay its last respects to those who had fallen during the February Revolution. A procession of delegates from all quarters of the city and from factories advanced toward the Field of Mars. We started out early in the morning, together with workers from the power stations. Entire families came out with their children. The funeral march thundered. The fragrance of spring filled the air and through its intoxicating freshness came the sound of many voices singing in honor of the fallen.

A column wound its way slowly down the Nevsky Prospect. A line of red coffins, covered with wreaths, seemed to flow high over their heads. We reached the Field of Mars when it was already dark. Torches flickered solemnly around the square and over the freshly covered graves as the silent procession passed by.

The February Revolution was over. A new chapter had begun. The elections for a new executive committee took place at the power station amidst scenes of exhilaration. The representatives of each party argued heatedly and obstinately for their cause. Father and Yablonsky spoke up for the Bolsheviks. The Bolsheviks won and held the majority on the new committee, on which Father was elected to serve. The chairman of this committee was Lazar Yablonsky.

Chapter Twenty-Two

A Room for Stalin

The first evenings in March always seemed to transform the streets of the capital. I could sense the strangeness of the March twilight as it fell on the wide St. Petersburg boulevards; I felt this with particular poignancy in the spring of 1917 in the city we now called Petrograd. The city itself appeared in a fresh guise, young and beautiful in some different way.

As I walked home in the evenings, I took in avidly all the details of spring in Petrograd. There is a militiaman, in a student's cap, who shifts awkwardly from one foot to the other. He is obviously unaccustomed to his new role; he lifts his arm with its makeshift red band sewn to his sleeve. A truck stops on a corner and is immediately surrounded by a crowd of young people.

There's going to be a meeting, I think to myself. Should I stop and listen? No! I hurry on. I must not be late for the family get-together. Father should be with us again soon; we see so little of him as he is immersed in his work on the executive committee and the power station. Mother will be late coming home, and as most of the household work now falls on me, I increase my pace as I hurry to the station.

Huffing and puffing, the train with its double-decker

carriages pulls up, and I climb into the upstairs part of the carriage. The little steam train gathers momentum as it rushes by Staro-Nevsky and speeds us toward the embankment. The Neva looks a trifle sullen at this point, as if it resents having to wash the gloomy little houses of the Nevsky Gates after having swept around the palaces and luxurious mansions farther up. I jump off the train at the stop where the Neva approaches the main buildings of the Thornton factory. Our three-story house stands opposite, with its repair shop belonging to the cable section which Father manages. I run up to the entrance and hurry into the house with that mood of elation which has never left me since the first days of the Revolution. One of the mechanics opens the door for me.

"Are any of my folks home?" I asked, looking around for their familiar overcoats. There is a man's thick black overcoat on a hanger which I do not recognize, and a long striped woolen scarf on a small side table.

"Who's the visitor?" I ask the mechanic.

"Stalin has returned from exile," he replies. "He's just arrived."[42]

Stalin! Joseph! He has returned! He is already in Petrograd! Yes, of course he wrote to Father on his return journey. We were expecting him, but even so news of his arrival rather startled me. I fling open the door quickly. Our guest is standing by the table. I remembered that he never liked sitting down for a long time, and even when he was talking, he liked to pace up and down the room. His movements are calm and self-possessed. And now that he has seen me, he takes a deliberate step in my direction.

"Oh, hello," Joseph says.

I had not seen him for four years, four years of cruel, lonely exile. Naturally he has changed, but it is difficult to say what precisely has changed. Is it his dress? No, he wears a dark suit, as usual, and a dark blue buttoned-up shirt. Perhaps it is the felt boots which I had never seen him wear before. No, it is his face which has changed, not only because he has grown thinner and his cheeks are sunken (doubtless from tiredness); he is still clean-shaven and his moustache is trimmed short as always. He is also as lean as ever, but his face has become older, yes, considerably older. His eyes are the same, and that mocking smile never leaves his lips—it is still there.

"Well, and how did you finally come to locate us?" I said, at last. "I really didn't expect to see you today."

Joseph takes his pipe out of his mouth—the pipe without which I could not imagine him from that day.

"Well, I did find you, as you see. Of course I went to your old address in the Vyborg district. They said you'd moved. . . . But what on earth made you live so far out of town? I came by train, and it went on and on. I thought I'd never arrive."

"We haven't been here long and are thinking of moving shortly. I hope you haven't been waiting too long. Father and Mother should be back soon," I babble on. It really was infuriating that our long-expected guest from such distant parts should have arrived and that there was no one at home to receive him properly.

"I must have been here an hour, or a little more, I'd say. Well, how are you all? Olga and Sergei? Where are your two brothers and sister?"

I tell him hurriedly that Pavel is at the front and that we have had no letters from him for some time. Fedya must have been held up somewhere and Nadya should be back from her music lesson shortly. Then I suddenly remember my duty as a hostess.

"I'm sure you must be hungry. Let me get you something. It won't take a minute."

"I wouldn't say no to some tea perhaps. . . ."

I rush out of the room toward the kitchen to get things ready, and there in the corridor I bump into Father.

"Joseph has arrived!" I shout as I rush past him into the kitchen.

Father goes into the dining room. I can hear excited

greetings and a torrent of questions. Father sounds so happy.

Just as I light the samovar Nadya appears in the kitchen.

"Who's here?" she asks out of curiosity; she has not even bothered to take off her little hat and coat.

"Joseph has arrived! Stalin!"

"Joseph!"

Nadya throws off her coat and goes into the dining room. When I come in to lay the table, the place is alive with laughter. Father, Mother, Fedya and Nadya have surrounded Stalin. There are great gales of laughter. . . . Stalin mimics the home-spun oratory of the speakers who came out to greet the exiles returning from banishment at provincial railway stations. He imitates them to perfection. You can see them choking with bombastic phrases, as they beat their chests and exclaim: "The holy Revolution, the long-awaited, dear Revolution has come at last. . . ." We all collapse with laughter.

"Come on, it's time to feed your guest," Father prompts us. Nadya and I return to the kitchen, and soon there is a plate of steaming sausages on the table, sausages which we found, to our great delight, in the larder.

We sit around the table for a long time listening to our guest.

Stalin tells us how he hurried back from Achinsk to Petrograd, where the February Revolution caught up with him. He was one of the first to arrive in Petrograd. Of course had he traveled from Kurieka the journey would have taken him longer, but he traveled with a group of exiles on an express train and reached Petrograd from Achinsk in four days.

Stalin tells us how he happened to be in Achinsk. In October 1916 the exiles were called up into the army. These recruits, including Joseph Vissarionovich from the Turukhansk province, were sent to Krasnoyarsk. They made their way there by dog sleigh or reindeer or simply on foot. During the breaks on the journey they made arrangements to meet their friends, but in order not to raise the suspicions of the authorities, they organized drinking parties; it was assumed that the army recruits were having a last fling with their companions before their induction.

But Stalin was rejected for military service.

"They thought I'd be an undesirable element in the army," he told us, "so they found fault with my arm."

Stalin's left arm could not bend easily at the elbow. He had suffered an injury in childhood. The elbow had then become infected, and as there had been no one to treat the lad, blood poisoning developed, and Stalin almost died.

"I don't know how I pulled through; it was either my strong constitution or the ointment prescribed by the village quack; anyway I recovered," he recalled.

But traces of the injury remained and it was this which gave the officials at Krasnoyarsk the opportunity to reject him. Stalin was sent to Achinsk to serve the remainder of his exile.

We ask Stalin to tell us about his exile in those far-away places where he spent so many years. He talks about the north, the tundra with its endless snow horizons and the frozen rivers where the sturdy good-natured natives sit for hours on end at an ice hole, fishing. He lived in one of their simple huts and gained their confidence, so they came to like him.

"They called me Osip and taught me to fish. It so happened that I began bringing in a catch larger than anyone else. Then I noticed that my hosts began whispering among themselves. One day they came up to me and said, 'Osip, you know the magic word!' I was ready to burst out laughing! Magic word, indeed! The fact is they chose a place to fish and sat there whether the fish rose to the bait or not, whereas I waited for the fish to rise, and if not, I went to another place, and so on until I got a good catch. I explained all this to them. But I don't think they believed me. They thought I had kept the secret to myself."

Stalin recalled the northern rivers: the Yenisey, the Kurieka, the Tunguska, whose waters merge in the distance with the calm, dreaming, silent northern sky.

"Once or twice I was caught up in a storm on the river. On one occasion I really thought the end had come, but I managed to scramble ashore. I did not think I'd succeed, but I did it. The river was rather too boisterous for my liking that time."

Afterward, Joseph Vissarionovich asked us about our experiences. He seemed interested in everything we had to tell him. The samovar had gone out a long time before, but we still sat around talking.

"What time are you getting up tomorrow morning?" asked Joseph. "I have to be at the *Pravda* editorial office early."

"We also have to be in town early, so we'll wake you up," we promised.

A bed is made up for Stalin in the dining room where Father also sleeps on the other divan. We go into the next room, our communal bedroom shared by Mother, Nadya and myself. But we do not feel like going to sleep. Nadya and I begin to whisper, going over stories we have just heard. Suddenly Nadya repeats a phrase of one of the railway-station orators whom Stalin had imitated so brilliantly, and we cannot control our laughter: we snort and giggle into our pillows. We know they are trying to get to sleep next door, but the more we try to suppress our laughter, the louder our shrieks become. There is a sudden knock on the wall. It's Father.

"Will you shut up, you little rascals! It's time you went to sleep!"

We hear Joseph's voice interrupt Father:

"Leave them alone, Sergei. They're young. Let them laugh. . . ."

Only then do we pretend that we have been shamed

into silence and lie still. But next door we can hear Father and Stalin discussing the activities at the power station and the regions with which Father is in contact. Father shares his problems and talks about some of his successes.

"We have many Mensheviks and Social Revolutionaries on the executive committee, so one has to put up a pretty hard fight."

"What's the workers' reaction to *Pravda?*" asks Stalin.

"It sells like hot cakes," replies Father. "We can't get enough copies."

We fall asleep to the sound of Father's deep, sonorous voice, interrupted now and again by Stalin's short, clipped sentences.

But we do not have the opportunity of waking our guest the next morning. He is up before any of us. We sit down to breakfast and hurriedly drink our tea. Fresh issues of newspapers are passed from hand to hand and we read about what is going on in the world outside.

"Hurry, hurry . . ." Joseph Vissarionovich chivies us along. Joseph, Fedya, Nadya and I climb to the top deck of a railway carriage of the old-fashioned little steam train which comes puffing into the station.

"And where, pray, are you off to?" asks Stalin. "Today is Sunday."

We explain that we intend to leave the apartment at the Nevsky Gates, which is so far from the center of town, and are going to look for a new apartment. There was an apartment for rent on one of the Rozhdestvenskaya streets which sounded as if it might be suitable.

"That's splendid," says Stalin approvingly. "Excellent. But you must put aside a room for me in your new apartment. You really must."

Just before he and Fedya leave us, Stalin repeats: "Now you won't forget, will you? You will put aside a room for me?"

Nadya and I found the advertisement about the apartment in one of the newspapers. The advertisement offered three rooms, a kitchen and bathroom. And now here we are walking down the tenth Rozhdestvenskaya street looking for the apartment.

We are somewhat taken aback by the magnificent entrance hall and the imposing head porter. Nadya and I are awe-stricken as we go up in the elevator to the sixth floor. But we sigh with relief once we enter the apartment. Everything here is to our liking. There is a spacious entrance hall, which is in fact a large, light room that could serve as a dining room and a bedroom for Father and Fedya. The other room, which seems gay and cozy would be ours; and finally, the third room, which stands separated from the others at the end of the corridor, looks as if it had been specially designed for Joseph Vissarionovich Stalin. He could get on with his work in these peaceful, comfortable surroundings. We begin to negotiate immediately with the landlady to secure the tenancy. The apartment at number 17, Tenth Rozhdestvenskaya Street is ours!*

Our few belongings were immediately transported to our new flat. Joseph Vissarionovich's room, which we had painstakingly cleaned and tidied, stood empty waiting for its occupant. But it so happened that an earlier occupant was Vladimir Ilyich Lenin.[43]

We each reacted to our new life in different ways. Mother continued working at the hospital, and Father, who was rarely at home, busied himself with his Party and managerial affairs. I was sent to work for the First Congress of Soviets. News came from Pavlusha from Novgorod where his regiment had been transferred that he had been elected secretary of the local Bolshevik Party committee.

I spent my days in the light and airy halls of the ancient military school (on the Vassilievsky Island), where the First Congress was shortly to be held. The arched

*This apartment is now a museum. [Anna Alliluyeva's footnote.]

walls of the building echoed intermittently with snatches of conversation, exclamations and footsteps as the delegates sauntered through the halls. I established myself in the offices of the Mandates Commisssion where I inspected the delegates' credentials and provided them with passes to the congress. The delegates continued to arrive and among them I spotted our old acquaintances from the Caucasus and Petrograd; they comprised workers, peasants, teachers and students, but the military predominated. I could recognize the yellow ribbon of the Cross of St. George [the highest prerevolutionary military decoration for valor] on their field shirts.

Meetings were held in the halls before the opening of the congress, at which Menshevik orators often spoke. On one occasion, it was rumored that Lenin was expected at one such meeting. The Bolshevik leader Lenin would make a speech! His name was familiar and dear to me. "Lenin!" the crowd repeated his name at the congress and in the streets. "Lenin!" His name was on everyone's lips in Petrograd.

Father went to meet Lenin at the Finnish Station. He told us how thousands of Petrograd workers came to meet their leader, and how Lenin captivated them and warmed their hearts with his simple words that were comprehensible to everyone, which he spoke from the armored train. Lenin said that political power should belong to the workers and peasants, and that those who worked should govern their own land.

"Lenin provided us all with the right kind of Bolshevik ammunition," said Father, adding, "Stalin was there, with him, with Lenin. They left the station together."[44]

I first heard Lenin speak from the platform of the assembly hall of the military school. I did not manage to get to the front ranks: people stood in a solid mass in the corridors among the chairs and at the entrance.

Squeezed on all sides by men in military uniforms, I found myself stuck at one entrance. Only a few fragmentary sentences uttered by Lenin reached me. Nor could I get a chance to see him properly as I was smaller than those standing in front of me. It was useless for me to try to see the face of the orator, but I did catch a glimpse of his impetuous gestures and the movement of his arm, which he stretched toward his audience.

I again saw Lenin on the platform at the opening of the congress on June 3. He replied to Tseretelli [one of the moderate socialist leaders], who had said that 'there is no political party which could say: give power into our hands.'

"There is such a party!" Lenin shouted from his seat before moving toward the speakers' rostrum.

He told the congress what a proletarian government should do once it had achieved power.

When Lenin paused for a moment during his speech, thunderous applause greeted him. The Mensheviks tried to smother and cut short his speech.

"Enough! You have overrun your time limit!" they shouted at Lenin from the presidium.

"Go on! Continue!" the audience in the assembly hall demanded.

Stalin and Sverdlov attended the opening session. They were among the first to arrive, together with Lenin. I saw them before the session started. The three of them entered the empty hall with its closely set Viennese chairs, and I watched them from a distance as they went forward and seated themselves in one of the front rows.

We had not seen Stalin for many days. And his room in our apartment still stood empty.

"We must call on him," Nadya and I decided. "Perhaps he has changed his mind about coming to live in our apartment."

The best way to find him was to go to the offices of *Pravda,* which we did early one evening. The small editorial offices were crowded and filled with cigarette smoke. Our attention was drawn to a thin woman who sat at one of the tables. Her face was extraordinarily attractive. Her rich chestnut colored hair was secured by two combs. She sat there reading a manuscript, wearing a dark dress with a high collar edged with white lace. We could not refrain from asking who she was.

"That is Maria Ilyinichna Ulyanova, Lenin's sister," they told us. Stalin was in another room. "He's busy," someone said, but we sent a message to him saying we would like to see him, and he came out to meet us.

"Well, hello," he said, smiling affectionately at us. "I'm glad you have come. How are things at home?"

"Fine," we said. "Everyone's fine. And your room is waiting for you. You remember the room you asked us to keep for you?"

Stalin's face again lit up with a smile and then suddenly clouded over.

"How very kind of you, but at the moment I have other things on my mind. I'm busy, terribly busy. But do keep the room for me. Most certainly keep the room for me."

Someone came up to him at that moment and Stalin hurriedly shook hands with us.

"Consider the room as mine," he said as we parted. "And give my regards to your mother and Sergei."

Chapter Twenty-Three

Lenin's Barber—Stalin

During the last days of the congress I hardly left the military school. I was busy writing, checking shorthand records and organizing the archives. In the evenings I arrived home pale and completely exhausted and immediately went to bed. In the mornings I could hardly make myself get up. Mother became alarmed:

"You're not well, Niura. You must see the doctor. Remember, your lungs are weak."

Mother reminded me that doctors had warned me about my lungs even when I was at school. But I had forgotten all about the warning, which was stupid of me. . . . Mother spoke to Father, and despite my protests, I was made to go to the doctor.

"Give up work immediately," he said, "and, better still, go out of town."

The doctor's advice scared my parents so they got together to decide what should be done. They had a Finnish friend, a train driver, who advised them to send me to Levashev, a village, to stay with some of his acquaintances.

When I left for Levashev our apartment on the Rozhdestvenskaya became quite deserted. Nadya was staying with friends near Moscow, and Fedya was working in the country, so Father and Mother remained alone in the apartment.

After the noise of Petrograd I was surprised at the peace which prevailed in the pleasant little summer resort of Levashev. I had left town at the end of June when the situation of the provisional government was very confused and popular discontent expressed itself in grumbling and general indignation which grew with the passage of time.

I tried to rest at Levashev, drank milk and sunbathed regularly, but somehow I could find no peace. I ran as often as I could to the railway station. Vague and conflicting rumors were circulating among the passengers as to what was happening in the capital.

"The Bolsheviks are being driven out. Kerensky will not let them take over," I gathered from snatches of conversation.

"Bolshevik demonstrations have been fired on.[45] But they won't give up. They have popular support."

I heard these remarks, pronounced either with malice or anger, and sensed the hidden menace, and my heart sank. Bolsheviks were being arrested, and demonstrations were being dispersed. What was happening to my people, to Father and Mother? They must have taken part in the demonstration. It was impossible to stay at Levashev much longer. Mother had intended to visit me, but she had sent a message through our friend the train driver to say that she had been held up and would not be able to come. That finally decided me. I quickly threw my things into a suitcase, looked around at the peaceful little houses of Levashev and boarded the crowded train.

Our progress was painfully slow. Passengers embarked and disembarked; they were mostly vacationers, some kind of petty officials or milkmaids with their pails. Among them were soldiers and sailors, some armed and some not.

Squeezed against a hard seat somewhere near the carriage door, I listened eagerly to their conversation. The situation in Petrograd predominated. Here were people of different social standing, holding contrary opinions, mostly complete strangers, airing their opinions and arguing about one thing only—what was happening in the capital.

References to Lenin and the Bolsheviks could be heard in every corner of the carriage.

"The Bolsheviks have been driven out. . . . Lenin has run away. . . . He's been shot. . . ."

I listen and grow alarmed. I refuse, I don't want to believe in what they are saying.

The passengers interrupt each other, trying to astonish each other with exciting versions which they have culled from "reliable sources."

"He's escaped, I'm absolutely sure. . . . He's in Kronstadt. He's been seen there."

"No, he was taken aboard a minesweeper. . . . A man I know told me."

I want to plug my ears, not to listen to this foolish gossip, but the train has already arrived at Petrograd. I jump off and run to the square where the Finnish Station is located. It is a warm, sultry July day. The city seems unexpectedly calm, familiar and quite ordinary. People hurry by, trams come and go. Can something be brewing behind this façade of everyday life in the streets?

I manage to push my way somehow on to a crowded tram. The conversation on the train is repeated. I grow more alarmed. Finally I reach the Tenth Rozhdestvenskaya Street. I pause for a moment to regain my breath and look through the heavy glass entrance door. Unperturbed, as if nothing had happened, the familiar porter sits in the hall. I try to sound calm:

"Are any of my people home? Have you seen them?"

"They seem to be in good shape. Everything's in order. Your Father's at home, I think."

Nevertheless my hand trembles as I press our bell. I am a little astonished because no one opens the door immediately. I ring again; the door opens slowly, halfway.

"Papa! It's me . . . Are you all right?"

Father does not reply immediately. Is he angry because I came back? He has a cautious expression on his face, looks around, and checks to see if the door is properly locked. Only then does he speak to me:

"Well, never mind . . . Let's go into the dining room. We have guests. Mother is here, too."

Oh, so that's what it is! We had guests! Some friends who have come to see Father, and I turn up so unexpectedly. I feel calmer now as I go to the dining room.

There are people sitting around the table. I have not seen them before.[46] But I immediately recognize the person to whom I am first introduced. He sits on a sofa in his shirt sleeves, wearing a waistcoat and a light-colored shirt with a tie (the rooms are unbearably stuffy on this warm day). He looks at me intently, screwing up his eyes.

"Vladimir Ilyich, meet my eldest daughter, Niura."

I make an enormous effort to appear calm and collected as I shake Lenin's hand.

And suddenly all the stupid gossip I heard on the train, the tram and in the streets, springs to my mind. He ran away to Kronstadt, he's hiding on a minesweeper! But he is right here, in our apartment on Rozhdestvenskaya, in the center of Petrograd! I decide to tell Lenin about all the stupid rumors I had heard.

"I really didn't expect to see you here. They were saying in the train that you had run off to Kronstadt, and that you were hiding on a minesweeper. No really! That's what they said . . . You were seen in Kronstadt and on the minesweeper."

"Ha ha ha!" Lenin laughs with infectious gaiety, leaning backward. "So they say I am on a minesweeper? That's splendid! A new version of my escape. I'm delighted that they saw me in Kronstadt. What do you think, comrades?"

Vladimir Ilyich makes me repeat everything I heard on my journey, what things I noticed in the streets and the general appearance of the city. After the pent-up emotions of the day, I relax completely, I chat and laugh and forget all about my fears.

Vladimir Ilyich is so simple, so courteous; he asks questions and listens with such evident sincerity that I am made to feel as if I were his equal.

'But he's wonderful, absolutely wonderful!' I tell Mother when we go into the kitchen.

"He's a splendid person. Splendid . . ." Like me, Mother finds it difficult to describe him. "He has been here since yesterday [July 6, 1917]. I met him at Poletayev's. They were saying that it would be dangerous for Lenin to stay here. Kerensky wants to arrest him. It was suggested that he should give himself up voluntarily, but he refused categorically.[47] Stalin is also opposed to the idea. So it was decided that he should stay in hiding for the time being. They are searching for him all over the city. It's fortunate that we have a new address and that no one knows it."

I ask Mother to tell me exactly how Lenin came to our place.

Mother had been the first to suggest that Lenin could best be hidden in our place. This was at Poletayev's apartment. The Poletayevs were well known and the police could come at any moment.

"But no one knows where we live," said Mother. "We've only been here a couple of months."

Mother had dropped in on the Poletayevs straight from her work at the hospital. She had not been home for a few days. So it was decided that she would first return to the apartment, see how things were at home and return to fetch Lenin. As there was no time to lose Mother came home immediately. She met Father in the entrance hall.

"Only we must be quite certain we can provide Lenin with a completely safe hiding place," Father said after he had learned what had been discussed at the Poletayevs.

When Mother returned, Lenin was waiting for her. She told him that everything was in order at home.

"You'll be absolutely safe at our place, Vladimir Ilyich. I'm quite convinced," she said.

Early next morning Lenin came by himself to our apartment. There was such a reassuring calm and confidence about him as he inquired about Mother's health with such touching concern that one would have thought that a friend had dropped in for a moment. He was so charming and gay. But his first question was:

"Olga Eugenievna, please show me all the entrances and exits to your apartment."

He was taken through the kitchen to the staircase leading to the tradesmen's entrance. Then he went up to the attic and glanced inside. Returning to the apartment, he again walked through all the rooms. And afterward he sat down on the sofa, and smiling, with a wicked expression in his eyes, he looked at Mother.

"Well, now, Olga Eugenievna, I won't budge, even if you want to throw me out. I like everything about your home." And suddenly he burst out laughing. "You know what struck me? I remember the faces of some of my friends whom I visited in these last few days. Their faces became very long and their eyes grew round with fear. Well, I immediately turned around and left."

"So he decided to stay at our place," Mother said, concluding her account. "We gave him Joseph's room. I think he'll be all right there. Joseph was here yesterday and we're expecting him now at any moment."

Joseph Vissarionovich came to see Lenin a couple of hours or so after my return home. They had tea in Lenin's room and talked together for a long while. Then Stalin had to go off on some urgent business. But before he left, he dropped into the kitchen and, taking Mother aside, said: "Well, what's the situation with provisions? Is Ilyich [Lenin] eating? Do the best you can for him." When Stalin left, Mother burst out laughing.

"Lenin says exactly the same thing about Stalin. 'How's

Stalin eating? Please look after him, Olga Eugenovna, he seems to be losing weight . . .' "

Whatever else, Mother did not have to be told how to look after her friends when it came to mealtime. She always approached Lenin's room as quietly as she could. He invariably left the door open. He would sit there at the writing table, reading and making notes, never lifting his hand from the paper, which he filled page after page.

Mother would wait for a few seconds on the threshold. If Lenin was engrossed in a book or was writing and did not notice her, she would leave to return some minutes later.

She would repeat her attempts to attract his attention a few times, until finally Lenin would lift his head. She would then address him quietly. But mostly Lenin would sense Mother's presence immediately.

"Olga Eugenievna, pray come in. You want to see me, my dear?" he would say in his inimitably courteous manner.

"Vladimir Ilyich, it's lunchtime," Mother would remind him softly but decisively.

"But really, Olga Eugenievna, I'm not hungry. You shouldn't have bothered. I'll go on working. There's so much to do."

"I'm sorry, Vladimir Ilyich, but you have to eat. I'll bring your lunch presently. Have a bite and then get on with your work."

Mother's voice sounded most determined. She would approach the desk and start moving the papers carefully to one side. Ilyich would look at her and smile good-naturedly.

"Is that an order?" he would ask, resigning himself.

"Absolutely," Mother would reply delightedly and go off into the kitchen to fetch a plate with food which had already been prepared.

Mother always observed most carefully everything Lenin did. From time to time she would peep into his room from the corridor to see if he required anything. Once she saw Lenin lift his head from his manuscript and pass his hands over his eyes with a tired, absent-minded gesture.

"Is there anything you want, Vladimir Ilyich? You've been working since early morning. You really ought to have a break and lie down—you only went to bed at dawn."

But Lenin had already taken up his pen.

"No, Olga Eugenievna, I must work. . . . I'll rest sometime later."

Mother was very distressed because she could not vary Lenin's diet. Food was getting difficult to obtain in Petrograd. Sometimes Father would bring some additional item of food and Stalin would bring something extra. We still had a reserve of dried peas which usually went in the preparation of soup or pease pudding. These Mother cooked as tastily as possible to feed Ilyich, our friends and anyone else who dropped in to see him or us.

We had to line up for bread, which was obtained with the greatest difficulty. But we had a supply of rusks which one of Pavlusha's friends brought us before Lenin came to stay with us. On one occasion I had a stroke of luck: I was able to buy a basket of strawberries in the street market. I remember that day very well because just as I was walking toward the market, I glanced around involuntarily, as I did habitually, and I noticed a tall woman in front of me. She came slowly toward me with a pensive expression on her face.

She was wearing a modest linen dress, and there was a small straw hat on her blond, graying hair, but I was struck by her forceful character and the great purity of her expression. I looked at her so intently that she herself appeared to be surprised. A sudden thought crossed my mind: Isn't this Vladimir Ilyich's wife? Nadezhda Konstantinovna must look exactly like her. I had heard our friends mention her name and knew that she would come to see Vladimir Ilyich one of these days, but I had never seen her or her photograph.

I turned around and looked at her again: "Surely this must be she?" I said to myself. I recalled that Pavel had told me about his encounter with Nadezhda Konstantinovna. The Novgorod Party organization had sent Pavel as a delegate to a regional Bolshevik conference which took place in May in the Kshesinsky Palace.[48] Pavel met Lenin there for the first time and heard him speak from the platform. Pavel was supposed to make a speech himself, but he was too scared to appear at such a large gathering and especially in front of Lenin, so he went and spoke to Krupskaya [Lenin's wife's maiden name], who was working in the Secretariat, which dealt with the reception of delegates. She was very sympathetic.

"She tried to encourage me. 'Don't worry,' she said. 'Keep calm,' " Pavel confided to me. And she immediately agreed to receive a written report from him, asking him to make it as detailed as possible.

I returned home in an elated mood because I had managed to buy a basket of strawberries. But when I brought it into the dining room I almost dropped the basket out of surprise. Sitting with Vladimir Ilyich at the table was the same woman I had met at the marketplace!

"I'm glad you turned up," he said. "Nadya, I want to introduce you to the daughter of our dear hosts."

I shook Nadezhda Konstantinovna's hand and offered her and Lenin some strawberries.

"Really, this is quite unnecessary," he protested. "Why spend your money? It's not necessary. . . . You'd better give the strawberries to Olga Eugenievna."

I finally persuaded him to take some strawberries. Lenin was always embarrassed if anyone made a fuss of him, and he did not like to trouble Mother or to ask me for the smallest favor. And he always expressed his thanks for the most insignificant things we did for him. And whenever he interrupted his work, he always dropped into the dining room or kitchen to have a friendly chat with Mother or me.

Talking to him in ordinary domestic surroundings, it was difficult to imagine that he was hiding from great danger and possibly even from death. He never spoke about it or showed any fear or alarm.

We spent one particularly anxious night. It was past midnight and we had all gone to bed. Suddenly there was a shrill ring at the tradesmen's entrance. Mother and I, who were sleeping in the kitchen, were the first to jump up. Who could it be? Everyone was at home and our friends had already left and no one was likely to visit us at that late hour, especially as entrances of the apartment house had been locked.

At that moment Lenin appeared, quickly but quite unperturbed.

"You had better open the door, Olga Eugenievna," he said. Mother came to the door softly. She hesitated for a moment and then asked: "Who's there?"

"It's me. One of us. Please, open the door." It was a woman's voice.

Mother opened the door; a woman stood on the threshold, holding a small suitcase in her hand.

"I have come from Moscow. I have a message for Lenin," she explained.

It was Nogina.[49]

For the first time I saw Lenin become angry.

"What kind of conspirator are you to behave like this?" he said. "Don't you understand you could have spoiled everything and got us all into trouble, including my hosts!"

Nogina tried to justify herself by saying that the message was urgent, but Lenin did not accept her explanations.

'All the same, you should have waited until morning,' he said, repeating all the rules of conspiracy. Later, when they went into Lenin's room, Nogina passed on the message she had been given by the comrades in Moscow.

Stalin came to see Lenin almost every day. On the first day that Lenin came to stay in our apartment, he visited him with Sergo Ordjonikidze.[50] Nogin and Stassova also dropped in. They discussed whether Lenin should give himself up to the provisional government. Both Stalin and Sergo were against this, because it was quite clear to them that Kerensky's promises could not be trusted.

"The Junkers [cadets] will kill Lenin before taking him to prison," said Stalin.

Once Maria Ilynichna [Lenin's unmarried sister] and Stalin came to see Lenin. This was on the day following the raid on *Pravda* by the cadets. Soon afterward, Poletayev's son Mikhail came in. Lenin came into the dining room and Mikhail Poletayev told him there and then, in my mother's presence and mine, that Kamenev had accepted Kerensky's proposals and that he (Kamenev) would be arrested that same day. It was also said that a police carriage would be sent to fetch him.

We felt that the news brought by Mikhail Poletayev had made a painful impression on Lenin.

"Olga Eugenievna, I should like to ask you a favor. Go to Kamenev and tell him that I insist categorically that he refuses Kerensky's proposals. Please go to him straight away."

Mother went. She returned in a most distressed condition which she could not hide and told me what had happened.

As she was going up the stairs to Kamenev's apartment, she met Nogin on the way down. He stopped Mother and said: "I can guess who you are coming from and why, but I think nothing can be done." He glanced upward. "They have already made up their minds."

Mother went upstairs and rang the doorbell. Kamenev's wife answered, but when she heard that Mother had come from Lenin, she was startled:

"No, no, you can't see Kamenev. He's not well. If you tell me what it's about I'll pass on the message."

Mother realized that she would not be allowed to see Kamenev; she therefore repeated what Lenin had said so insistently. Kamenev's wife replied with hostility:

"Kamenev knows what he's doing. He doesn't need any teachers."

She then disappeared into a room. Through the half-closed door Mother could hear her convey Lenin's message, and then exclaim hysterically: "You must never agree to it! We are in mortal danger. If you don't accept Kerensky's offer straight away, we shall all perish!"

She then turned from threats to begging. Afterward she came out and told Mother coldly that Kamenev had already accepted the provisional government's proposals as the authorities had been informed, and that he was giving himself up that day.[51]

Lenin listened to Mother's account without any indication of protest or anger. He merely shrugged his shoulders and said: "I had almost expected as much . . ."

He then went into his room.

Our address had become familiar to too many people and the chance of discovering Lenin's whereabouts increased daily. It was then that the idea was mooted that Lenin should go to Sestroretsk [a small town on the Gulf of Finland], to a village called Razliv. Father, who had worked in that region for many years, knew every corner of it.

"I'll take you there, Vladimir Ilyich," he said. "I know every side turning there." And he began to list all the streets and junctions which one should follow.

Lenin nevertheless insisted on a carefully drawn up plan of their escape route. Father provided such a plan on the following day, and both he and Lenin studied it carefully. On the evening of that day [July 24, N.S.] Lenin left our apartment.

Stalin came in shortly before the departure, and everyone gathered in Lenin's room to devise a way of disguising him so as to make him unrecognizable. Mother suggested bandaging Lenin's face and forehead. At first this proposal was accepted and Mother began to bandage Lenin's head with a wide gauze. But when Lenin looked at himself in the mirror, he told Mother to stop.

"No, Olga Eugenievna, don't bother. I'm more likely to attract attention with this bandage. It's not worth it."

The bandage was removed.

"Wouldn't it be better if I shaved?" Lenin suggested. "Take a look at me when I am without my beard and moustache."

Everyone agreed, and a moment or two later Lenin sat with his face covered with soap. Joseph Vissarionovich acted as barber. Without his beard and moustache Lenin was unrecognizable.

"And now let me try on your cap," Lenin asked Father.

It had been previously suggested that Lenin should wear Father's cap and coat. Lenin looked very much like a Finnish peasant with the cloth cap pulled over his eyes and Father's overcoat sagging over his shoulders. Lenin left the apartment accompanied by Stalin and Father. Each went his separate way, with Stalin and Father walking some distance behind Lenin.

Everything went as planned. They reached the Primorsky [Maritime] Station undisturbed, and from there Lenin boarded the train crammed with vacationers and went to Razliv.

Chapter Twenty-Four

Stalin the Lodger

The room which had been set aside for Joseph Vissariono-vich at Rozhdestvenskaya Street finally received its occu-pant after Lenin had left, despite Stalin's reservations.

"I should very much like to move in with you," said Joseph Vissarionovich, "but I don't think this is the right time. The apartment could be put under police observa-tion, and you might get into trouble because of me."

"Please don't worry about us, Joseph, we're accustomed to such things," Mother answered. "I'd be only too happy to have you in the apartment, but if it's dangerous for you, then of course we ought to hold things off for a bit."

But when Joseph Vissarionovich dropped in about a week later, Mother told him decisively: "No one seems to be keeping watch on the house. You'd better come to live with us, rest and sleep properly, and generally lead a more normal life."

And so Joseph Vissarionovich came to stay with us.

The day he moved in Stalin appeared to be more preoccupied than usual. He arrived late in the evening and retired to his room immediately after drinking tea. When we went to bed we heard him pacing slowly up and down his room. He must have fallen asleep much later, judging by the light which was still switched on in his room. In the morning he joined us at breakfast. Drawing a glass of tea toward him, he said, smiling: 'Well, I haven't had such a good sleep for a long time.' He then turned to Mother as if he had just remembered something.

"Now don't worry if I don't come to sleep here for a night or two. I shall be very, very busy, and besides, there's no harm in taking precautions."

In actual fact he did not sleep at our place for several days. Sometimes he would drop in in the evening or early morning to change his clothes, drink a cup of tea and snatch a brief rest in his room.

Stalin's arrival in our apartment coincided with the opening of the Sixth Party Congress [July 26, 1917], which took place in semi-legal circumstances*. Kerensky's secret agents shadowed the participants of the congress and watched members of the Central committee especially closely. Stalin, who made a report to the congress, had to be particularly careful. That is why he absented himself from the apartment during those days and dropped in only to steal a brief rest from time to time.

All his belongings were packed in a small wicker basket which he had brought with him from exile. In it he kept his manuscripts, books and a few items of clothing. He had only one old-fashioned suit which had become threadbare by now. Mother once tried to mend his jacket, but after examining it carefully, she said: "Joseph, you can't go around in this shabby suit. You must get yourself another one."

"Yes, I know, I know all about it, Olga. But I haven't time for such things. Now if only you could help out . . ."

So Mother and Aunt Manya made a round of all the shops and found a suit which fitted Joseph Vissarionovich exactly.

Stalin appeared to be delighted with the suit, but he

*The congress opened in a building belonging to the Sergievsky brotherhood on the Sampsonievsky Boulevard, and was later transferred to a school building at the Narvsky Gates, where the present House of Culture is situated [Anna Alliluyeva's footnote].

asked Mother to fit a chest protector into the jacket. He was having trouble with his throat at the time and did not like wearing collars and ties. Manya, who was very clever with her hands, made him a couple of black velvet protectors with a high neck, which he wore.

The apartment came alive when Fedya returned, followed by Nadya, who arrived from Moscow at the beginning of the school year.

She wanted to know about everything which had gone on during her absence and to share her own impressions with me.

"Imagine! Lenin stayed with us! How fortunate you were to meet him!" Then she suddenly burst out laughing. "You know, in the country where I stayed people were also divided into two groups. Those who were opposed to us invented all kinds of fairy stories about Lenin and the Bolsheviks. Whenever I went by, they would try to insult me. 'Just look at that Bolshevik there! No wonder your Father is one of those who is hiding Lenin!' "

Nadya was delighted to see her piano again, sat down, played a few favorite pieces and went off to bed early, exhausted by her journey.

Nadya enjoyed domestic work and liked to keep the house spic and span. The next morning she got up early and started heaving the furniture around and cleaned out the dining room and bedroom.

Stalin, who must have been disturbed by all the commotion, poked his head out of his room: "What's going on here?" he asked, surprised. "What's all the noise?" Then he saw Nadya in her apron, with a brush in her hand. "Oh, it's you! A real housewife has settled down to work!"

"Is there anything wrong in that?" Nadya bristled.

"Go right ahead. If the place has to be kept tidy, keep it tidy. Show 'em all how it should be done."

Soon after drinking tea with us in the morning, Stalin left the apartment until evening. Nor did he return to his room every night. Father was frequently absent and Nadya and I would sit up until the small hours waiting for them to return.

I was now working at the Smolny [Smolny Institute: Bolshevik headquarters] and we knew that the Bolsheviks were going from strength to strength. When I returned home in the evenings, Nadya would ask me impatiently: "Who spoke today? What did you hear? What are our comrades saying?"

Nadya was still at school, but she found high school tedious and boring. She could not concentrate her thoughts in the classrooms where the school girls repeated stale anti-Bolshevik gossip. She had long outgrown those enthusiastic little fans of "darling" Kerensky, but she knew it was pointless to try to change their minds. Most of the school children had undoubtedly been influenced by their parents and repeated the things they had heard at home: "The Bolsheviks! How awful! What do they want? They want to destroy everything!"

What could they have known about the Bolsheviks and what they fought for? But one could not say this aloud at the time. It was better not to attract attention to oneself or to the house which persons hunted by their enemies used to visit. But Nadya made no attempt to hide her convictions.

"Now I've been definitely labeled as a Bolshevik!" she once told me. "You see, the girls suddenly decided to make a collection in aid of some government officials who had been treated unfairly. . . . They came around to my class and everyone was expected to make a contribution. They came up to me, but I proclaimed loudly: 'I won't make a donation!' They looked somewhat surprised.

" 'What do you mean you won't make a contribution? Did you leave your money at home?'

" 'No, I've got some money, but I won't spend a penny on any governmental officials!' You should have seen the commotion! They all began shouting at me: 'She's a Bolshevik! That's what she is—a Bolshevik!' I was delighted. Let them know what I am."

I was not always able to satisfy Nadya's understandable curiosity. Routine office work at the Smolny obscured the main issues of the day and it was difficult to grasp exactly what was happening every day. That is why we waited for our elders to return to put us into the picture.

Father told us about the situation in the Vyborg, Vassilievsky and Nevsky Gate factories and his growing conviction of the influence and authority of the Bolsheviks. Joseph Vissarionovich was particularly anxious to get all the details; he advised Father on his next course of action and what words to use to bring over the waverers and the faint-hearted to our side.

We listened to what Stalin had to say and grasped the immensity of the work which was being done by the Bolsheviks. Sometimes Stalin did not come for some days. We would stay up at nights waiting for him to return, but when we finally lost all hope and went to bed, there would be a knock at the door.

"What, are you already in bed?" we could hear Stalin's voice. "Get up, you sleepyheads! I've brought you some roach and bread!"

We would jump up, dress hurriedly and rush into the kitchen to make tea. Often we went into Joseph's room so as not to awaken our parents, who were sleeping in the dining room. And the atmosphere in his room immediately become carefree and noisy. Stalin would crack jokes and caricature all the persons he met that day, sometimes kindly, sometimes maliciously. At home, the target for some of his mild jokes was a country girl called Panya who came to stay with us. She spoke in a northern dialect, pronouncing her *o*'s roundly, and was in the habit of saying: "We come from Skopsk, we do!"

"Oh, you come from Sk-o-o-psk, do you?" Stalin would laugh, making his *o*'s as round as Panya's. "And what makes you talk like that, you people from Sk-o-o-psk? Come on, tell us."

Panya would lift her apron to her face and giggle: "Oh, you are a one! You're always joking!" And to everyone's huge enjoyment, she would repeat: "Of course we come from Skopsk!"

Stalin liked inventing nicknames for people. He had his own favorite collection of these. When he was in a particularly good mood, he used to address us as "Yepifani-Mitrophani."

"Well, Yepifani, what's new?" he would ask.

Sometimes when he would poke good-natured fun at us or rebuke us for not carrying out an errand properly, he would say: "Oh, you're a Mitrophani, that's who you are!"

"Tishka" was another favorite word of his. He told us that this was the name of a dog he had house-trained while he was in exile. He loved talking about that dog.

"He used to keep me company," Stalin told us. "During the long winter evenings—if I had any oil for the lamp—I would sit reading or writing, and Tishka would run in from the cold and lie down, pressed against my legs, growling as if trying to say something. I'd bend down, ruffle his ears and say something like this: 'Well, Tishka, are you frozen? Had enough running around? Warm yourself now. Warm yourself.' "

Stalin also told us of the visits his friends the Ostyaks paid him during the long polar evenings.

"One of them used to come more frequently than the others. He would squat on the floor and stare unblinkingly at my oil lamp. He seemed to be drawn to the light. He could sit there on the floor the whole evening without uttering a single word. I would give him my pipe to suck from time to time. That was a great treat for him. Then we would dine together on frozen fish. I would clean and scale it there and then and Tishka would get the head and tail."

As previously mentioned, Stalin used to catch his own

fish, stocking up during the warmer days. But even in winter he had to replenish his reserves. Fishing tackle had to be fixed at the ice holes and markers set up. Once during the winter, he set out with fishermen to check the catch. The grounds were several kilometers away. When they reached the river, they separated and Stalin went on alone. The catch was excellent, and Stalin heaved a string of fish on his shoulders and made his way back. Suddenly a snowstorm blew up as a blizzard approached. The polar night mist was impenetrable, and the frost grew sharper all the time. The load of frozen fish grew heavier on his shoulders, but Stalin refused to unburden himself. He knew that to part with the fish would mean to condemn himself to starvation. Fighting his way against the wind, Stalin pressed on. The markers on the ice had long disappeared, covered under the snowdrift. Still Stalin marched on, without any signs of human habitation in front of him. Could he have lost his way?

Then suddenly, quite close to him, he saw shadows and heard voices.

"Hey, you there!" he cried out. "Wait for me!"

But the shadows sprang aside and disappeared and their voices grew still. All he could hear above the roar of the snowstorm were the frozen fishes knocking against each other on his back. His strength was almost exhausted but he continued to walk. It was certain death to stop. And the blizzard continued. When he was about to give up all hope, he suddenly heard the bark of dogs. A whiff of smoke reached him. Dwellings at last!

Feeling his way with his hands, he reached the first hut and, bursting in, collapsed on a bench. His hosts jumped up the moment he appeared.

"Osip—is that you?" they asked, pressing themselves against a wall in terror.

"Of course it's me. Who did you think it was, a goblin?"

"We saw you outside and thought you were a water demon! So we became frightened and ran away. . . ."

There was a sudden crash on the floor. The crust of ice which covered Stalin's face had fallen on the floor. That is why the fishermen had been scared. He had appeared with his face covered in ice, with icicles hanging from his head and body, looking just like a water demon! And those frozen fish rattling behind his back! Stalin could not help bursting out into laughter as he saw the embarrassed faces of the Ostyaks who surrounded him.

"I slept eighteen hours at a stretch after that," he said, concluding his story about the blizzard.

Sometimes, during our evening tea parties in his room, Stalin would come up to a swivel bookcase near his bedside and pull out a volume of Chekhov.

"It would be rather nice to read something. How would you like me to read you 'A Chameleon'?"

He greatly admired "A Chameleon," "Unter Prishibeev" and other stories by Chekhov. He read, stressing all those incredibly funny remarks made by Chekhov's characters. We would shriek with laughter and ask him to read more. He often read from the works of Pushkin and Gorky to us. He particularly liked and knew almost by heart Chekhov's short story "Dushenka" ["The Darling"].

"That woman is a real 'Dushenka,' " he would say about one of our acquaintances, using Chekhov's own epithet.

When he talked about the most serious and most important matters, he could always see their funny side. His humor was sharp and colorful whether it related to people or events. I recall his story about a meeting of the Central Committeee when it was decided whether Lenin should give himself up or not; it was often retold in our house. Stalin portrayed how the temperamental Sergo Ordjonikidze grabbed a nonexistent dagger in his hand and exclaimed: "I'll stab anyone with my dagger who wants Lenin to be arrested!"

Stalin was equally friendly with the young people who

gathered in our house, Fedya's friends, or Nadya's and my girlfriends.

No matter how late he came home, Joseph Vissarionovich always sat down to work after one of our tea parties or after he had had a word with Mother and Father. But tiredness soon began to tell and that is why perhaps Joseph Vissarionovich acquired the habit of lying down for a brief rest before sitting down to his desk. Puffing away at his pipe, he would concentrate in complete silence before suddenly getting up, and after a few turns up and down the room, sit down at his desk. Once he fell asleep with a lit pipe in his hand. He woke up to find the room filled with smoke; there was a smoldering hole in the blanket made by the pipe.

"This is not the first time it's happened to me," he said with annoyance. "No matter how hard I try I suddenly drop off to sleep."

In September, a Democratic Conference opened at the Alexandrinsky Theater, in Petrograd. I again worked in the Mandates Commission at this conference. There were some happy encounters with our Caucasian friends. Two days after the conference opened, Stalin brought home a comrade from the Caucasian group whom we did not know. Stalin introduced us to him.

We looked with curiosity at our guest, who shyly shook hands with all of us, smiling with his large kind eyes. He was of medium height, squarely built, with smooth black hair and a pale, lusterless face. He spoke with a pronounced Caucasian accent. Stalin said: "This is Kamo. You just listen to him—he's got plenty of interesting stories to tell you!"

So this was Kamo, the hero of such legendary exploits! Stalin loved to tease him gently: "Do you know why they call him Kamo? It's because he always says 'Kamu? Kamu?' [To whom? To whom?]."

Kamo only smiled at Stalin's jokes.[52]

Joseph left his guest with us, adding as he went: "You must ask him to tell you all about his adventures!"

Kamo stayed with us the whole evening and we did not notice the evening go by, we were so gripped by the adventures of this truly romantic revolutionary. Today his story is widely known from his biography, but at that time we were really shaken by his description of his half-fantastic life.

He took part in the famous expropriation of the Tiflis State Bank and was arrested in Germany. In prison he feigned madness and fooled even the most experienced German doctors. He spent many years behind bars and organized several courageous escapes. We were touched by his story about a sparrow he tamed in prison. Kamo spoke a lot about Stalin and then his calm, quiet voice became exalted. Stalin was Kamo's first teacher.

Kamo told us in great detail about his attempt to escape from the Kharkhov prison where he was incarcerated when the Revolution broke out. He had intended to simulate death and escape after he had been taken to the mortuary. But the February Revolution released him from prison. We had the impression that he was a trifle disappointed because he could not carry out his daring plan of escape.

Then he began to talk about the future.

"There will have to be a lot more fighting before we seize power," he said, but he had no doubts that the Bolsheviks would win.

Epilogue

Anna Alliluyeva's pennultimate chapter ended with the prophecy made by Kamo that the Bolsheviks would have to do more fighting before they could seize power. This was true of the long-term future when the civil war broke out in earnest, but the October Revolution (October 25, O.S.) was a comparatively bloodless affair in the capital as numerous witnesses, including Anna Alliluyeva, have testified. At 2:04 on the morning of October 25 all resistance in the Winter Palace, the last stronghold of the Kerensky government, had been broken. The occasion was "not devoid of comic touches like the bombardment of the Palace with duds from the cruiser Aurora," *as Isaac Deutscher has written.*[53] *Stalin's participation in the uprising in any case was minimal. Even Anna Alliluyeva's account, doctored by her editor and approved by the censors, gives little additional information as to what he was doing on that famous day. She met him on one or two occasions in the corridors of the Smolny and exchanged some elevated gossip about the heroism of the armed workers who were storming the Winter Palace. Her record is interesting in that she provides a few personal touches of how she and her sister Nadezhda spent that particular day which changed the entire fate of Russia and the world and brought Stalin nearer to the pinnacle of absolute power.*

The Bolsheviks would, of course, win: we had no doubt of that. We knew that in the Vyborg district where Uncle Vanya lived and whom we often visited, the workers were demanding openly the transfer of power to Lenin's party. The Sampsonievskaya district was also on the boil. People listened only to Bolshevik orators; it was better for Mensheviks not to put in an appearance.

"Lenin will soon arrive," they said on the Vyborg side; "then everything will be different."

But Lenin was not able to return to Petrograd as yet. We knew that he had left Razliv for Finland. One morning just before the October Revolution there was a ring at the door. When I opened the door I saw a smallish man, dressed in a black overcoat and a Finnish cap standing on the threshold. He was clean-shaven except for a small moustache, but his features did not appear familiar to me.

"Whom do you want to see?" I asked cautiously.

"Is Stalin at home?"

I immediately recognized Lenin from his voice.

"Good Lord! You look just like a real Finn, Vladimir Ilyich!"

"Yes, it's quite a good disguise." Lenin laughed and repeated his enquiry. "Is Stalin home?"

Mother looked out into the corridor and exclaimed joyfully: "I'm so happy to see you, Vladimir Ilyich." Lenin embraced her, and they exchanged greetings.

Stalin came out of his room, having heard Lenin's voice, and Mother invited them both into the dining room for a meal, but Lenin refused. After a brief conversation Stalin and he left together.

In the tense pre-October days the whole network of plans was drawn up in the Smolny which led to the events on that autumn day of October 25: Lenin, who still could not appear openly, invisibly followed the execution of his orders.

I saw Stalin at the Smolny, but he appeared at home more rarely. Occasionally he would ring up from the porter's lodge at the entrance.

"I shall be dropping in today," he would say to anyone of us who answered the telephone. "I might even come in early. Will you be at home?"

"Come as soon as you can," we said, knowing very well that he had not slept for several nights.

"I'll be with you in an hour, perhaps."

But an hour went by and he had not turned up, and we sat waiting up for him. He was delighted to find us all in the dining room.

"We were getting worried," Mother said, greeting him. "What kept you? Life's so uncertain these days, anything could have happened. . . ."

"You shouldn't worry about me," he replied in a mock serious voice. "I've more reason to be concerned about you, Olga Eugenievna. Kerensky should have grabbed you long ago for the kind of speeches you make at the hospital!"

"You're always joking," Mother said, insisting on her point. "Just look at yourself; you've grown so thin. It's not right."

But he would continue to joke and Mother would give up amidst the laughter which followed.

Stalin often spoke of the magnificent ordinary folk of Petrograd—workers, soldiers and sailors—whom he met. He found qualities of great human courage, simplicity, all the qualities of unassuming heroism. He would repeat some episode or a snatch of conversation which he had heard, and then would say: "With such people one can accomplish anything. . . ."

I recall that he came home on the eve of the October Revolution, took off his leather jacket and cap (which he always wore at the beginning of autumn) and came into our room. We were happy to see him. After taking tea and listening to what Father had to say, he said calmly: 'Yes, everything is ready. We take action tomorrow. All military forces are in our hands. We shall take power. . . .'

After the October Revolution when Lenin and his collaborators had established the Soviet government, Stalin came home just as cool and collected as before. He spoke of the events of October 25, praising people's courage and the greatness of their accomplishment. He also told us how the Telephone Exchange had been seized by sailors of the Baltic Fleet.

"They advanced like men of iron. . . . Cadets were shooting down at them from the windows and bullets mowed them down one by one, but they came forward without flinching. Splendid people! Splendid! Real Russian people."

That evening [October 25], the second All-Russian Congress of the Soviets was due to open at the Smolny Institute. It was already known that the majority of delegates belonged to the Bolsheviks. Worker and peasant delegates kept arriving at the Smolny, and I scrutinized their passes and showed them their places. My feeling of anxiety turned into confidence of victory. . . . I had been told that Lenin had arrived at Smolny and that he would be speaking for the Bolsheviks.

I had promised to take Nadya to the opening of the Congress, but this meant that I had first to run home to fetch her. It was already dark as I hurried through the streets, clutching her pass in my pocket. I was struck by the silence in the streets and the absence of people. It had begun to drizzle and a chill autumn wind pierced one's bones.

I found Nadya alone. After grabbing something to eat, we ran into the street into the impenetrable darkness. The street lamps were not lit. We walked along the tram lines, covered in wet snowflakes. There was no one else about. Suddenly a shadow loomed before us. An old man was walking along the tram track, with a dog trailing gloomily behind him, his walking stick echoing on the cobbles.

"Hope your dog doesn't bite," we said, glad to have met up with someone at last.

"Don't be afraid. She doesn't bite," the old man replied. "Where are you girls off to on a night like this? There's trouble in town, fighting outside the Winter Palace, they say."

"We've things to attend to, grandfather," we said.

The old man turned into a side street and we were alone again, but as we approached Smolny Square we saw brightly lit windows, and we showed our passes to the guard and were allowed into the building. For a moment we were blinded by lights and stunned by the commotion and noise, but we pushed our way through the crowd into the assembly hall, looking for familiar faces.

Judging by the excitement and cheers we guessed that something very important had happened, and there, suddenly, in the crowd streaming toward us, we saw Stalin. He stopped and beckoned to us: "Oh, it's you! Delighted you're here. Have you heard the news? The Winter Palace has just fallen and our men are inside!"

On the next day, October 26, I saw Lenin at the congress. It was as lively as on the previous evening, and the columned hall where the meeting took place was crowded, with a solid wall of bodies crammed in the corridors and entrances.

Menshevik orators still made attempts to be heard, but the audience refused to listen to them.

"Clear out! Get out of the way!" the delegates shouted.

And there was Lenin, his simple familiar self, dressed in his worn black suit, coming onto the rostrum.

"Lenin! Lenin!" the delegates shouted, applauding deliriously, their faces transfigured with joy. They were seeing him after a long absence when the things he had foretold had been accomplished.

The hall grew silent.

With his inimitable gesture, Lenin stretched his hand forward and declared: 'The proletarian revolution in Russia has been accomplished . . .'

NOTES

(1) See Beria, Lavrenty: *On the History of Bolshevik Organizations in Transcaucasia,* Foreign Languages Publishing House, Moscow, 1939; pp. 20-21, for a list of persons participating in these early Marxist circles. Sergei Alliluyev is mentioned among these. Beria was Commissar for Internal Affairs (1938-1945) and later Deputy Prime Minister in charge of security (1941-1953). He was either executed or assassinated some months after Stalin's death in 1953, accused of being an "imperialist spy."

(2) The name Stalin "first appeared in January 1913 below a long article in the magazine *Prosvescheniye* (*The Enlightenment*) devoted to a study of Marxism and the national question." (Payne, Robert, *The Rise and Fall of Stalin,* W. H. Allen, London, 1966, p. 141.)

(3) See Deutscher, Isaac, *Stalin, a Political Biography,* Oxford University Press, 1949, pp. 30-31.

(4) Serfdom was abolished in 1861 during the reign of Emperor Alexander II (1818-1881).

(5) Black Hundreds: name given by their opponents to the extreme right-wing organization known as the Union of the Russian People, which advocated anti-Semitism, unquestioning support for the autocracy, and organized pogroms against Jews, students and working-class organizations.

(6) The theological seminary in Tiflis "was a breeding ground for rebellion," according to Payne (*op. cit.*, p. 43).

Stalin entered the seminary in September 1894 and was expelled as "politically unreliable" on 27 May, 1899 (see Yaroslavsky, E: *Landmarks in the Life of Stalin*, Lawrence & Wishart, London, 1942, p. 18). In December 1893 the seminarists went on strike. Among the eighty-seven seminarists who were expelled was Lado Ketskhoveli, one of Stalin's closest friends. (Payne, *op. cit.*, p. 44.)

(7) Victor Kurnatovsky (1868-1912) "became a legendary hero of the revolution of 1905" (Deutscher, *op. cit.*, p. 36). In 1906 he was arrested and sentenced to death for the part he played in forming the so-called Chita Republic. His sentence was commuted to penal servitude for life. He succeeded in escaping to Japan and later went to Australia. "In the autumn of 1911 V. Kurnatovsky came to Paris, a sick man. Here V. I. Lenin devoted special attention to him, helped him with money, saw to it that he entered a hospital and had the care of the best doctors. But he could not be saved. On 19 September, 1912, V. Kurnatovsky died." (Beria, *op. cit.*, pp. 22-23.) But according to Payne (*op. cit.*, p. 67), Kurnatovsky grew weary of violence and "became a moderate socialist, and there was the inevitable break with Lenin."

(8) Gleb M. Krzhizhanovsky (b. 1872), an engineer: exiled with Lenin, later developed electrification in Russia.

(9) Leonid B. Krassin (1870-1926), an electrical engineer. According to Payne "it amused him to place his intelligence and his considerable fortune at the service of the Bolsheviks, to collect money from sympathetic liberal friends, to forge identity papers, and to manufacture bombs." (Payne, *op. cit.*, p. 113.) He also opposed Lenin's 'dictatorial methods' within the party, 1904-1905, and had him expelled from the Central Committee. (See reference: Everyman's *Concise Encyclopaedia of Russia,*

Utechin, S. V., Dent, London, 1961, p. 290.) He later (1918) became Commissar for Trade and Industry; between 1922 and 1926 he was twice ambassador to Britain and once to France. He died in London in 1926.

(10) Yaroslavsky (*op. cit.,* p. 38) quotes the newspaper *Kavkaz* (*The Caucasus*) as stating that apart from the illegal press discovered by the police, other items such as "blasting gelatine and other paraphernalia for the manufacture of bombs, a large quantity of illegal literature, the seals of various regiments and government institutions, as well as an infernal machine containing 15 lb. of dynamite" were also found. Some twenty-seven persons were arrested. Stalin himself was detained for questioning, but released, according to Payne (*op. cit*., pp. 104-105).

(11) The Fifth Congress of the Russian Social Democratic Party was held in May 1907 in the Brotherhood Church, Southgate Road, London. Stalin attended this congress under the pseudonym of Ivanovich: it was his first and only visit to Britain. His credentials were challenged by the Mensheviks, but he was allowed to attend without any voting rights. (See Deutscher, *op. cit.,* pp. 90-91, and Payne, *op. cit.,* pp. 111-112.) Although he was entitled to speak he made no attempt to do so. Although his official biographer Yaroslavsky claimed that "at the Fifth (London) Congress, Stalin continued to expose the fraudulent intrigues of the Mensheviks" (*op. cit.,* p. 56), there is no record of his intervention. He did, however, write a report of the congress proceedings (*Notes of a Delegate*) on his return to Georgia. "It was at the London Congress that Koba (Stalin) first met his future great rival (Trotsky)," says Deutscher (*op. cit.,* p. 91). Trotsky, however, claims to have no recollection of such a meeting. (See Trotsky, Leon: *Stalin,* Hollins and Carter, London, 1947, p. 90.)

(12) See Trotsky (*op. cit.,* p. 475) for a list of seventeen of Stalin's aliases and pseudonyms.

(13) Stalin may have been married to his first wife, Ekaterina Svanidze, at this time. Trotsky states (*op. cit.,* p. 86), "It is possible that the wedding took place in prison (1903). Such cases were not rare. It is also possible that the marriage took place only after his flight from exile at the beginning of 1904. . . . If Koba's wedding took place after his exile, it can in part explain his political passivity during 1904." Payne dates the marriage on June 22, 1904. Ekaterina Svanidze died in 1907, possibly from pneumonia, and was buried according to the rites of the Orthodox Church. (Payne, *op. cit.,* pp. 100-101.) Her brother Alexei Svanidze perished in the purges, according to an account attributed to Khrushchev (*ibid.,* p. 710).

(14) "In 1897, Vera Vietrova, a student imprisoned in the Peter and Paul Fortress, burnt herself alive after soaking her clothes in lamp oil. The student body was deeply shaken. A wave of meetings swept over every university in the country." (Kerensky, Alexander: *The Kerensky Memoirs,* Cassell, London, 1966, p. 24.) Similar acts of self-immolation took place from time to time, to which Anna Alliluyeva refers.

(15) On January 22, 1905 (known as "Bloody Sunday") a young priest, Father Gapon, led an unarmed demonstration of workmen to present a petition to Tzar Nicholas II. The crowd was fired on by infantry and charged by cavalry, killing some two hundred person. The official *History of the Communist Party of the Soviet Union* (Bolsheviks, Moscow, 1945, p. 57) accuses Gapon of being a paid police agent, but Kerensky (*op. cit.,* pp. 46-47) throws some doubt on this statement. Lenin's wife, Nadezhda K. Krupskaya, gives a sympathetic portrait of Gapon in her *Memories of Lenin* (1893-1917), Lawrence and Wishart, London, 1942, pp. 84-85. The massacre on "Bloody Sunday" signaled the beginning of the 1905 revolution.

(16) Deutscher, *op. cit.*, p. 68.

(17) The Tzar's October Manifesto promised "to grant people the unshakable fundamentals of civil liberty, based on principles of true inviolability of the individual, freedom of conscience and speech, and the right of assembly and union." (Kerensky, *op. cit.*, pp. 55-56.) According to Deutscher, however, "It was too half-hearted to satisfy the opposition; and it was so obvious a sign of weakness that it was bound to encourage fresh demands" (*op. cit.*, p. 77).

(18) "Kamo's" real name was Semyon Ter-Petrosyan, the son of a prosperous Armenian businessman. He was responsible for 'expropriating' a quarter of a million rubles from a Tiflis bank in June 1907 and transferring the money to the "Bolshevik treasury abroad" (Deutscher, *op. cit.*, p. 87). For a full account of Kamo's exploits, see Payne, *op. cit.*, pp. 115-117. Stalin's part in this affair has never been fully explained, but as Deutscher states (p. 88), Caucasian Mensheviks "apparently had an inkling of his true role, for they tried to impeach him before a party jury for contravention of the ban on raids imposed by the last congress". Stalin, however, removed himself from Tiflis to Baku and escaped such a "trial."

(19) Sergei Alliluyev in his memoirs gives the figure of slain as twelve.

(20) In June 1905 the cruiser *Potemkin* went over "to the side of the revolution." See *History of the C.P.S.U.* (B), *op. cit.*, pp. 60-61. "The other vessels of the Black Sea Fleet did not join the revolt of the *Potemkin*. Having run short of coal and provisions, the revolutionary battleship was compelled to make for the Rumanian shore and there surrender to the authorities."

(21) Capital punishment had been abolished as early as

1754; a court-martial, however, could apply the death penalty in cases of treason and other state crimes. See *Concise Encyclopaedia of Russia*, *op. cit.*, p. 86.

(22) Anna Alliluyeva confuses this Georgian daily with the *Chveni Tskhovreba* (*Our Life*) of which only thirteen issues were published between February 18 and March 7, 1907. See Beria, *op. cit.*, p. 52. *The Akhali Tskhovreba* (*The New Life*) appeared in twenty issues between June 20 and July 14, 1906 "under the direction of Comrade Stalin" according to Beria (*ibid.*). It was suppressed by order of the Tiflis governor-general.

(23) According to Payne (*op. cit.*, p. 719) this statue of Stalin has now been removed but "a recent visitor to Georgia found the massive square pedestal still in place, with the inscription: TALIN. Someone had attempted to erase the name, and having obliterated the S he had grown weary of the task."

(24) It is not clear from the text whether Anna Alliluyeva refers to Yakov, Stalin's eldest son by his marriage to Ekaterina Svanidze, or to Vasily, his son by Nadezhda Alliluyeva, but it is probably the latter. Yakov was brought up by his grandparents in the Caucasus (Deutscher, *op. cit.*, p. 127) and perished in unknown circumstances during the Second World War in which he served as a lieutenant in the Red Army. (Payne, *op. cit.*, p. 100.)

(25) See Preface, p. xv.

(26) See Beria, *op. cit.*, p. 87. Colchis: ancient Greek designation for the western part of the Caucasus to which the Argonauts came in search of the Golden Fleece.

(27) Piotr Stolypin (1862-1911), Russian statesman and prime minister, assassinated in 1911.

(28) Sergei Alliluyev's memoirs concluded with this story.

(29) "Stalin is a good fellow, but too much of an individualist in everyday life, while I believe in a semblance of order. . . ." (Payne, *op. cit.,* p. 152, quoting a letter from Sverdlov.)

(30) See Payne, *ibid.,* p. 34 for a description of Stalin's father, Vissarion Djugashvili. He died in Tiflis in 1890 when Stalin was eleven years old. (Deutscher, *op. cit.,* p. 4.) Stalin is reputed to have hated his father for the beatings he received.

(31) "This, incidentally, is Stalin's only private non-political letter we know. . . ." (Deutscher, *op. cit.,* p. 128.) The year the letter was sent is not stated. (Payne, *op. cit.,* p. 158 places it in 1915.)

(32) See Krupskaya, *op. cit.,* p. 196; also Deutscher, *op. cit.,* p. 117 and p. 124.

(33) May 5, 1912 (N.S.), Stalin's fifth arrest, according to Beria, *op. cit.,* p. 201.

(34) Two hundred and seventy of the strikers were shot down, and two hundred and fifty were wounded. A general strike throughout Russia followed. (Payne, *op. cit.,* p. 142.)

(35) Payne, *ibid.,* notes Stalin's liturgical style. "Stalin never forgot the rhythms of the liturgical chants he heard as a choir boy and seminarian," Payne wrote.

(36) A Jewish workman, Mendel Bayliss, was accused and tried of ritual murder (1911-1913) but was acquitted after a storm of protest from liberal opinion both inside

and outside of Russia. Stalin's well-known anti-Semitism may have provoked Anna Alliluyeva to mention this case.

(37) Grigori Rasputin (1872-1916), a Siberian priest and mystic who exerted a pernicious influence on Nicholas II and the Tzarina. He was assassinated by relatives of the Tzar and a prominent right-wing member of the Duma.

(38) Anna Vyrubova, a close friend of Rasputin.

(39) Demian Bedny (1883-1945), a poet who enjoyed widespread popularity in the 1920's.

(40) Tzarina Alexandra Fyodorovna (1872-1918), daughter of the Grand Duke of Hesse and Queen Victoria's granddaughter, murdered with her husband and child by the Bolsheviks in 1918.

(41) V. M. Purishkevich, a right-wing member of the Duma who took part in the assassination of Rasputin.

(42) March 25, 1917 (N.S.).

(43) Between July 6 and 11, 1917; see next chapter.

(44) "Sergei Alliluiev said he saw Stalin leaving the Finland Station after Lenin's arrival, but he was the only eyewitness." (Payne, *op. cit.,* p. 177.) Lenin's wife, Krupskaya, makes no mention of Stalin's presence (*op. cit.*, pp. 257-258).

(45) These rumors were inflated. The so-called July Revolt initiated by Kronstadt sailors fizzled out, but "most Bolshevik leaders, including Lenin, thought themselves more thoroughly defeated than they actually were." (Deutscher, *op. cit.,* p. 151.)

(46) Although Anna Alliluyeva does not mention the fact, Zinoviev (executed in 1936 by Stalin during the purges) was also hiding with Lenin in her father's apartment. See Krupskaya, *op. cit.*, p. 272.

(47) Krupskaya (*ibid.*, p. 272) states that Lenin "wavered" and "argued that he ought to surrender to the authorities." But later that evening Stalin and others urged Lenin not to appear in court "and finally convinced him. . . ."

(48) Former residence of the Tzar's mistress, the ballet dancer, Kshesinskaya.

(49) Victor Nogin's wife. Nogin was a member of the Bolshevik Central Committee. Anna Alliluyeva does not disclose the nature of the message which Nogin's wife brought so urgently to Lenin.

(50) A close supporter of Stalin. Khrushchev stated at the 20th Party Congress (1956) that Ordjonikidze had been compelled to commit suicide by Stalin in 1937.

(51) Kamenev's wife, Olga, was Trotsky's sister. Both Trotsky and Kamenev were arrested but were released after about three weeks.

(52) Kamo, it appears, spoke Russian badly. Instead of saying *"Komu otnesti?"* (to whom should I take it?) he would say: *"Kamo otnesti?"* Hence the nickname given to him by Stalin. (Payne, *op. cit.*, p. 113.) (See note 18 and Preface.)

(53) Deutcher, *op. cit.*, p. 166.

DK
254
.A55
T8

1968